Memories of the Islands

The Life, Place, and Times of the Barber Family

by

Jasper E. Barber

authorHOUSE®

AuthorHouse™
1663 Liberty Drive
Bloomington, IN 47403
www.authorhouse.com
Phone: 833-262-8899

Published by AuthorHouse 04/13/2021

ISBN: 978-1-4343-0586-2 (sc)
ISBN: 978-1-4343-0587-9 (hc)

Library of Congress Control Number: 2007902750

Print information available on the last page.

This book is dedicated to my mother, whose love, devotion, and sacrifice for her family was as steadfast as the North Star, and whose life was the greatest sermon I ever witnessed.

Table of Contents

PART II

Acknowledgements

The information about family and related events covered in this book came from many sources. The friendly folks in the Family History Center of the Church of Jesus Christ of Latter Day Saints in Goldsboro, North Carolina, got me started. The staffs in the Register of Deeds and the Clerk of Court Offices in the Martin County Courthouse were very courteous and helpful in assisting me to navigate my way through their files, which produced a wealth of information. *The Enterprise*, Martin County's bi-weekly newspaper, was an invaluable source to which I am extremely grateful. Some of their stories shed light on my family's history that was news to me. I have gladly given *The Enterprise* credit where it is due.

Other sources of information include the North Carolina Department of Corrections, the Martin Memorial Library in Williamston, and numerous people in the community who took the time to share something they remembered.

My sons, Dean and Larry, suffered through the first draft; and my high school classmate Alton Hopewell took on the challenge of editing the final draft. I am indebted to Brian Strickland, freelance photographer in Goldsboro, for making the old family photos look new again.

To each of my sources and contributors, whether cited here or elsewhere in the text, I offer my sincerest appreciation for your assistance.

And I thank God who has sustained me with good health, a vision, and the wisdom to fulfill my dream.

Preface

I have discovered that one must do the same thing to a book that one does after planting a field of corn, peanuts, or soybeans: you must chop the grass and weeds out of it. I have been doing that to this book since the first draft, and like those fields I used to chop, I'm sure I have failed to do a thorough job. If you should happen to find more, please pluck them out and keep on reading.

This book does not follow the standard operating procedure of how books are to be written and assembled. You may read Part 1 from beginning to end, or you may read it from the end to the beginning, or read only the chapters that interest you. Part II is family data, of interest only to those related to the Frank Barber family.

Writing this book has been a challenge that I have struggled with for many years. I have always wanted to record the history of my family and life on the family farm. I wish I had started asking my parents questions and writing down the answers when I first learned to write. But like most people who yearn to learn their family roots, I waited until my primary sources were dead. My parents did not reveal much information about their upbringing or their relatives. Since I never asked, perhaps they assumed I was not interested. Some of my parents' relatives would visit occasionally, and we would visit one of their kin occasionally, but I really never knew where my parents came from or anything about them. I have not uncovered much, but each new piece of information I have discovered only adds to the number of questions I had when I started! While family data is limited, what I have found has given me a much greater appreciation of their sacrifices and accomplishments under far more difficult circumstances than I had imagined.

However, this book is about more than my family. I have tried to capture life in one small spot on the Planet Earth during one brief moment in history as I saw and experienced it. It is about the places and people I knew, some of my family's struggles, stories and anecdotes.

Another reason for putting this all together is because I believe it is important to know something about one's family. If my offspring and other family members will add to what I have gathered, perhaps it will give them a sense of where they came from and how we are connected. And I hope it will provide some inspiration for them to go beyond where we have been and what we have accomplished in life.

This book was not written with malice toward anyone, nor is anything included that is meant to embarrass or degrade anyone. I have taken the liberty of adding to the factual information in places to make the story more readable and as true to the times as my imagination would permit.

May you find as much joy in reading it as I did in putting it all together.

Jasper (Jay) E. Barber

PART I

Chapter 1 –
Boyhood Images

Rising before the sun comes up and working until after it goes down for the day, plowing horses and mules, riding in carts and wagons on dirt roads, the smell of honeysuckle in the spring, swamps, water rising and falling, a canoe made from a cypress tree, old houses used for barns, clapboard farm houses and tenant farmers, poor people and uneducated people, playing marbles, feeding mules and horses, cows, hogs, chickens, ducks, cats and worthless dogs, gathering eggs, untangling goats caught in wire fences, bouncing a half-gallon jar filled with cream on a pillow to make butter, milk that smells and tastes like wild onions, eating clabber and biscuit seasoned with sugar, hog killings and eating fresh cracklings and sweet potatoes, barbecued pork and family reunions on the Fourth of July, deerburgers, the smell of my mother's cooking drifting across the garden to the barn on a summer breeze, getting three of the best home-cooked meals a day any kid could ever ask for, watching mom wash clothes in winter on a washboard when she had cracks all over her hands, my mother's joy of getting her first washing machine, watching dad take honey from the beehives and eating fresh honeycomb, digging sweet potatoes on a sunny day in November, priming tobacco and hanging it in a tobacco barn, removing cured tobacco from a barn at three and four in the morning, hands covered with tobacco gum, grading and tying tobacco into bunches, tobacco auctions, big and small stacks of peanuts dotting the landscape, watching German prisoners of war dig and stack peanuts, picking peanuts with a Benthall peanut picker, bailing peanut hay with a baler operated with the power of a mule, using a peanut popper to shell peanuts for planting, gathering corn by hand, the annual cleaning of the chicken coop and outhouse, sugar cane taller than the mules, sugar cane being squeezed from the stalk and the smell of the cane juice being turned into molasses, the old black gentleman Mr. Nichols who cooked the molasses, shucking, husking and shelling corn before taking it to the grist mill for grinding into corn meal, cutting broom straw used for making brooms to sweep the house, plows—two-and-one, five-hoe, throwing, and cotton—oxen pulling logs out of the swamps, the roar of a Farmall tractor, pulling my end of a crosscut saw, trees that produced nuts or fruit—mulberry, walnut, pecan, peach and plum— sitting on a limb in a tall sweet gum tree eating fox grapes or sitting in the mulberry tree in the backyard eating mulberries, the tart taste of crab apples, playing in a hay loft with other kids, fishing at Devil's Gut and Rattling Gut Ditch, listening to the distinct sound of a pileated woodpecker or squirrels chattering, walking to the school bus stop on a frosty morning, crossing Daffin Swamp in a canoe enroute to school, riding to and from the school bus stop with my brother on a bicycle, riding a bike for the first time, being baptized, our first refrigerator, getting electricity and running water, currying cockleburs from the mules, riding a mule bareback, riding to town with dad in a wagon filled with watermelons and listening to him sing the watermelon song to attract customers, walking barefoot in hot sandy soil, stumping my toe on a clod of dirt in the bottom lands, the feeling of a summer breeze cooling my sweat-soaked body, the pure joy of drinking a glass of tea with ice in it on a hot day in July, breaking open a watermelon and eating the heart out of it with dirty hands, paddling a flat bottom boat through the swamps to get to my favorite fishing hole, hunting coon, squirrel, rabbit, deer, turkey, quail and dove, watching a hunting party clean and divide a deer after the hunt, taking a cold shower behind the mule stables, and saying good-bye to mom and dad, my boyhood, life on the farm, and wandering out into the world to find myself.

Chapter 2 –
Looking Back

There are some things that cannot be left behind, no matter the distance or time. Yesterday, today and tomorrow are tied together like Father, Son and Holy Spirit.

There was nothing extraordinary about the place where I grew up or my family. And yet, I have found no other place like it, or any people like my family. Not that I want it to, but my past will not go away. I grew up during hard times thinking my family was among the poorest people in the world, but when I revisit those days nearly six decades later I can celebrate them with a heart of thanksgiving and a new appreciation for the sacrifices my parents made for me and my siblings. And the knowledge I have acquired in that world beyond the one I grew up in has revealed that my self-diagnosis on poverty was incorrect. Compared to the rest of the world, I was truly blessed.

I cannot take today's generation back to the place of my youth, it is not the same; in just over a half century the people and the place have all changed. Most of the equipment used on the farm can now be found in museums, and the way in which crops were planted and the land tilled have long been outdated. The only livable home on the farm is the one in which I grew up and it has been renovated and the clapboard siding replaced with brick. Where once stood clapboard tenant farm houses are mobile homes and the occupants are no longer tenant farmers or farm hands. A new day has dawned and a new generation of people inhabits the land. The small farmer and the old ways of producing crops have all but disappeared from the landscape, replaced by farmers with huge tractors and machines that do most of the work. All that's left of those days are memories.

While it was all happening I did not realize that I was among a generation of people who were seeing the end to one era on the family farm and the ushering in of a new one. That era when animals provided the power needed to till the soil for crop production had lasted thousands of years. On the farm where I grew up, that era ended in the 1950s.

I was like a bird perched in the top of a tree: I could see all around, but I could not see myself or my place in history. During my first 18 years my world was limited to within 10 miles of where I was born, rarely escaping for a weekend trip to Hopewell, Virginia, to see my sister Hilma and her family or to Roanoke Rapids, North Carolina, to visit with my brother Arthur and his family. While doing my share of chores on the farm, I learned that sweating keeps your pores open and clean, and if it were possible to die from working too hard my mother would have died long before I was ever born. There I dreamed of the world beyond the one I was in and longed to explore it in hopes that it would be better.

It is near the end of the journey into that other world that I look back. I can clearly see myself growing up among the sparse forest of people that inhabited the sandy ridges surrounded by swamps in that part of the Roanoke River Basin called the Islands in Martin County. My childhood dreams, like the trees and bushes along the edges of the fields that reached out for the sun, motivated me to reach beyond my station in life. No doubt that other world I entered was a better place for me, but I cannot help as I reminisce that the place and the people of my youth are due far more credit for my success than I can imagine. It is a place I have visited often in my memory, and each visit has been as rewarding as the breezes that cooled my sweat-soaked body on hot summer days working in that good earth.

The story of my family and that place begins with my mother.

William Frank and Icelene Barber, c. 1931.

Chapter 3 –
A New Journey Begins

The memory of that winter, during the second year of the Great Depression, still haunted Icelene. It was not the weather that had made it so bad. It was what she had done to survive.

At times it seemed that survival was all there was to life. Her grandparents had settled in Bear Grass, North Carolina, during the 1870s. They were tenant farmers and raised three sons and two daughters. Her mother, Mozella, the fourth offspring of that union, married Joseph H. Davenport when she turned 18. Her brother, Joe Sammy, was born on June 20, 1896, and she was born on September 9, 1902. The marriage ended in divorce, and about all Icelene knew about her daddy is that he was not a good husband or father. For unknown reasons, Joe took her brother and left him with his mother to raise, and he disappeared. She remained with her mother, who married William Thomas Gardner on September 4, 1907. Her stepfather was a farmer, too, who lived just a few miles from Bear Grass. Life had been good in the Gardner home where she gained two half brothers and a half sister. And there she learned to read and write.

The one word that summed up the total of her life experiences was work. Her little bit of schooling had been a blessed relief from the manual labor that confronted her every waking day. She worked in the fields and family garden, planting, hoeing, and harvesting crops; she cooked and cleaned house; she learned to make clothing; she took care of people's children and cared for the sick. There were no chores on the farm or in the house that she had not learned to master.

At the age of 19, she returned to Bear Grass when she married Raleigh C. Bailey on January 1, 1922. He was 51 years old and had six children by his first wife who had died. Before his death in 1926, Icelene and Raleigh had two daughters, Kathleen and Hilma.

It was a struggle after his death to care for the family. When Raleigh died he left Icelene and the children with little more than the clothes they owned and a few pieces of furniture. At his death, Bailey's real estate was valued at $2,000.00 and personal property at $400.00. Dennis Bailey, the administrator of the estate, charged $800.00 for his services. The remaining $1,600.00 was divided among Icelene and his eight children. They each received about $170.00

That money had long been spent by the summer of 1931 when Frank Barber came into Icelene's life. He was an older man, too, almost 55, with a gang of children and no wife to care for them. She was 29 with two young daughters, and she had no prospects for a husband and saw none on the horizon.

She had agonized for some time over Frank's proposal to marry him. She could honestly say she was not in love with him, but then she did not dislike him either. He seemed honest in telling her about the death of his wife and the kids that were still in the home, being cared for by the older ones. Unlike her first husband, Frank was paying the mortgage on the house he lived in and a rather large farm. She did not know if Frank really loved her, either, but what she did know is that the two needed each other right now, and perhaps the love would come later. Her decision to accept Frank's proposal was based on the realization that she had two children that needed more in life than what she could give them, and on that one memory of the previous winter.

A late northeaster in March had brought a foot of snow and freezing temperatures that lasted for almost a week. The cupboard was near empty and the fields were frozen. Normally at this time of year, she could get a job plowing fields for spring planting. Icelene did not like to beg, though her neighbors would have provided for her had she asked. But her neighbors were some distance from where she lived and she and her daughters were hungry. They had not had any meat to go with their boiled potatoes and cornbread for three days.

As she sat by the woodstove wondering what to do, she saw a number of sparrows in the backyard, scratching under a bush near the outhouse for food. "If I could catch some of those birds," she thought, "they would make the taters taste a lot better."

She put on her coat and went outside and got a shovel and cleared the ground of the snow where she had seen the birds. Then she went to the tobacco barn for a bundle of tobacco sticks and some used tobacco twine. With the tobacco sticks she constructed a trap shaped like a pyramid and tied the sticks together with the twine. Then she tied pieces of the twine together so it was long enough to attach to a stick to hold up the trap and reach the window by the woodstove where she could pull it, dropping the trap over the birds once they entered. She took corn from the barn and shelled and ground it into small pieces to attract the birds. She put some of the corn just outside the trap and the rest under it and went back into the house and sat by the fire and waited for the birds to return. She did not have to wait long. In just a few minutes, the hungry sparrows descended upon the food, unaware of the trap. She pulled the string, causing panic among the birds.

She got up, ran to the trap, and through a small opening at the top reached inside and began retrieving the sparrows one at a time, breaking their necks and tossing them into a bucket. She counted them. There were 19. She took the birds back into the house and Kathleen and Hilma sat by the fire and removed the feathers while she gutted them. She cooked the birds and they ate all of them that night with their Irish potatoes and cornbread.

Icelene had gone into the woods with her 12-gauge Ivanhoe shotgun many times and killed rabbits, squirrels, and coons, and she could chop the head off a chicken or duck without a second thought. But when she looked back on her one and only feast on sparrows she felt remorse at having to resort to killing one of God's smallest creatures to stop the hunger pains. She had not forgotten the cries of terror and the sounds of the wings of the sparrows beating in a valiant effort to escape from the trap as she reached in to grab one.

No, she did not want to experience that again. So she had said yes to Frank's proposal, in spite of her own reservations and against the wishes of her mother. And on November 22, 1931, after they were united in marriage by the justice of the peace in Williamston, she and her new husband loaded all of her worldly possessions in Frank's wagon and she and her two daughters set out on a new journey in life.

It was not a real cold day, but it was cold enough. The clear blue sky and the sunshine made it feel warmer than it was. It was a good day for farmers to gather corn or dig sweet potatoes. This was the kind of day Icelene loved; she could work hard and still not sweat. But riding in a wagon pulled by two mules made it a bit chilly, even though she had on her overalls and denim jacket.

She was saying farewell to her beloved Bear Grass, North Carolina. It was a small crossroads community where a few families had settled in to eke out a living farming. The land was rich and the people neighborly and hard working.

As they rode past the Bear Grass School, she wondered if her daughters would get to go to another school, and she thought of the people she was leaving behind—her brothers and sisters, and all her friends in Bear Grass. Although the Islands were only a few miles from Bear Grass, she had never been there, and she wondered how long it would be before she would see her family and friends again. She had heard plenty of stories about the Islands, but did not believe the place could be as bad as everyone claimed. People had joked that the land in the Islands was so poor that a rabbit had to carry a cabbage under each arm to cross it. She suspected that story was about as true as her brother Simon's claim that he bought a new pair of shoes in Williamston and wore them out riding the mule home.

When they reached Number 90 Station, a combination gas and grocery store on Highway 64 east of Williamston, Frank stopped the mules and asked if they wanted anything to eat or drink. Besides a few snacks, Frank purchased five gallons of kerosene for the lamps and lanterns.

The road from Number 90 Station to the Moore Farm was nothing but a cart path, just wide enough for a pair of mules and a wagon. About half a mile from the highway, they went down a hill and into a swampy area. Limbs from the trees on each side of the road reached out and touched each other, forming a canopy that in summer kept the sun from reaching the ground. Many of the mud holes in the road were repaired with limbs and poles tossed across them, making for a bumpy ride as the wheels of the wagon rolled over them. For nearly two miles back into the low lands, the road only got a little better when they crossed a hill before going back into another swamp. The swamps were not completely filled with water, which made the trip a little less exciting. It was possible for motorized vehicles to enter the Moore Farm, but only when the swamps were dry.

The ride through the swamps was slow and uncomfortable, but enjoyable, too. There was a beauty and a smell about the swamps that was different from anything she had experienced in Bear Grass. Sunbeams easily penetrated the almost leafless forest canopy, alternately providing tiny amounts of shade from overhanging trees, limbs and bushes, and rays of bright sunlight, falling upon the wagon and its passengers with the steady rhythm of a heart beat. The fresh autumn air and the beauty of the forest seemed to wash her mind of the fears and anxiety she had about her second marriage, and for a moment at least, she felt at peace with herself.

Suddenly, the forest canopy opened up as the mules departed the last swamp and pulled the wagon onto the Island known as the Moore Farm. Besides forest and swamps, all she had seen since leaving Highway 64 were some open fields and a few dilapidated houses occupied by black families. A hundred yards from the edge of the swamp was the place she would call home for most of the rest of her life.

A road ran from north to south through the middle of the huge farm, named the Moore Farm after a previous owner. At the north end of the farm was a path through the forest to Devil's Gut. Beyond that was the Roanoke River, the dividing line between Martin and Bertie Counties. She was awe struck for a moment to think that she was now married to a man who owned all this land.

As the wagon pulled up in front of the house, she saw kids everywhere, in clothes that needed washing and mending. And they all looked like they were starving. The home stood in the middle of the farm with several pecan and walnut trees nearby. A mulberry tree was in the backyard. Part of the yard was bare sand and part was covered with brown crab grass. On one side of the house stood a neatly stacked pile of split pine stove wood for cooking and beside it a pile of firewood for heating the home. The two-story clapboard house was recently built, but it had no luxuries. There was no plumbing; the outhouse was located 50 yards behind the house, inside a fenced-in lot that included a chicken coop. The smoke house was behind the house and beside it was the garden with a wire fence around it. Growing in the garden were collard greens, turnips, and rutabagas. It brought to mind the story someone had told her of the rabbits having to carry their own food to cross the farm, but from all that she saw, there would be no shortage of food in this place for the rabbits or the family. She could see three other homes on the farm, one nearly a half a mile south down the road through the middle of the farm and another located some three or four hundred yards east across a branch, visible only because the trees had lost most of their leaves. The third home was at the north end of the farm. The homes were occupied by Frank's older sons or daughters and their spouses and children who were tenant farmers.

She could not help but notice how quiet it was. And at the time she did not know that the only sounds she could hear of the outside world would come from an occasional airplane or a train blowing its whistle as it traveled the railroad tracks between Jamesville and Williamston on the far side of Highway 64. A battery powered radio would be their only connection to the world outside the Islands, and it would be used sparingly for news and weather reports.

As she surveyed her new place of abode, she was sure there was never a slave who was expected to do all the work that awaited her. But there was no turning back; there was nothing to go back to; and despite the hard work that lay ahead, there was hope of better days for both families. She knew in her heart that not every day would be filled with sunshine. But it was falling upon her today, and for that she thanked God, who she believed would get her through the stormy days as well.

Her spirit was high as she got down from the wagon and met the rest of her new family for the first time. There was Robert, 19; Harry, 16; Ben and Major, twelve-year-old twins; Clyde, 10; Emily, 8; and Henry, 5. Her daughters Kathleen and Hilma were 9 and 7, respectively. She and her children were in a new and different world from the one they had loved and left in the small community of Bear Grass. She had arrived in the land of necessity at the beginning of some of the darkest days in American history—the Depression was gaining momentum.

Her trip from Bear Grass to the Moore Farm had taken less than half a day. For Frank, it was a much longer journey.

Chapter 4 –
The Barbers Move to Martin County

The Barber family moved to Martin County, North Carolina, sometime before 1850. Henry and Mary Emily Barber showed up on the 1850 census and were the first family of Barbers to settle in Martin County. They were farmers in Jamesville Township and, between 1847 and 1852, they had three daughters and a son, Benjamin T. Barber, born December 26, 1848.

Though they did not own any slaves, Henry enlisted in the Confederate Army on June 17, 1861, at the age of 40. Whether he was a volunteer or forced to join is unknown, but military service was not a career the Barbers pursued. Private Barber served with Company H, 1st Regiment, North Carolina Troops, Infantry. The unit was known as the Bagley Guards. The sketchy records of the period reveal that Henry died in Lynchburg, Virginia, in February 1863. The cause of death is unknown.

His only son Benjamin married Emma Gardner on March 8, 1873. He was 24 and she was eight days away from her 18th birthday. The roots of the Barber family in Martin County would be firmly established through this couple. They had four daughters and eight sons. They also were farmers in Jamesville Township. The third child and first son of this union was William Frank Barber, born December 27, 1877.

Frank would almost double his father's production of children and establish a colony of Barbers in the Islands Section of Martin County. He married three times and had two sons by his second wife's sister. His first wife, Jessie, whom he married around 1895, died while giving birth to their first child, which also died. Her death occurred after the 1900 census was taken. Frank and Jesse lived near his parents' home in Jamesville Township.

Frank married Lizzie Rowena Simpson in the home of her parents, Major and Margaret Simpson, also of Jamesville Township, on September 11, 1901. Lizzie was one day shy of her 19th birthday and Frank was 23. Before she died at the age of 49 of cancer of the stomach on May 22, 1931, she gave birth to 16 children: 12 survived; one daughter, Lizzie Margaret, died at age four and one twin and one set of twins died at birth. Why Lizzie's sister Gertie was living in their household is unknown, but between 1909 and 1912 she and Frank produced two illegitimate sons.

Frank's third wife was Icelene Davenport Bailey. When they married on November 22, 1931, he was almost 55 years old and she was 29.

Most of the Barbers who were born in Jamesville Township stayed in Jamesville Township. Although there are no boundaries to mark its location, the area in which they lived became known as Barber Neighborhood because so many of them lived in the area.

Jamesville Township was and still is a farming community. Back then land owners and tenant farmers raised most everything they ate. They sold their tobacco, peanuts, corn, and soybeans, hogs, chickens, and cattle to purchase goods they needed for their farming operations and the necessities of life. Farmers did not amass fortunes; they survived from year to year, and got ahead or fell behind based on weather conditions and the demand for the goods they produced. Job opportunities for the uneducated, and most were lacking a formal education, were limited to farming or other back breaking occupations such as logging, fishing or carpentry.

Frank was among the few who chose to leave Barber Neighborhood, though it took him a few years to find a place to settle down

After their marriage Frank and Lizzie lived in Jamesville Township. They moved to Norfolk, Virginia, where they lived for a while, but exactly when that occurred and how long they stayed is unknown. A number of deeds in which Frank and Lizzie are named indicate they may have lived in the Jamesville community most of the time between 1901 and 1917 when they moved to the Islands Section of Martin County.

In December 1903, Frank and Lizzie purchased 292 acres of land from John C. and Sarah Getsinger in Jamesville Township for $300.00. Between 1905 and 1909, they sold the land in five smaller blocks for $685.00.

The obituary for Tillie Barber Barnes, one of Frank and Lizzie's older daughters, noted that she was born in Norfolk, Virginia, in October 1904. If this is correct, then the land purchased in 1903 could have been rented to someone or placed in the care of a tenant farmer. The fact that Frank and Lizzie purchased the land does not mean they had to live on it, so it's possible that they lived in Norfolk for a number of years. Some of the other older children also told of traveling between Norfolk and Jamesville, but none of the obituaries of the others listed Norfolk as their place of birth.

One story Frank told to his younger children had its setting in a bar in Norfolk. He said a Marine came up and slammed a beer down in front of him. Frank said he hit him just once and he didn't get up. A second and a third Marine followed with the same results. Frank had some tattoos on his arms. It is unlikely that he got those in the small town of Jamesville in the early 1900s. There is no record of his serving in the military. Frank was an excellent blacksmith, a trade he could have learned most anywhere, but one that would have been useful to him in Norfolk and on the farm.

In 1911, Frank and his brothers Warren and Hoyt and wives sold a 20-acre tract of land to Emmaline Barber for $20.00. This was their mother, and the land probably had been willed to them by their father.

Frank paid poll taxes in Jamesville Township in 1912, but there is no record of his paying this tax again in Martin County until 1916 when he paid it in Williams Township. His whereabouts between these two dates are unknown, but he and his family would soon find a permanent home.

Chapter 5 –
The Move to the Islands

There is no question about where Frank and Lizzie and family lived from 1917 on. On November 7, 1916, he signed an agreement with W.S. Hadley in which Hadley conveyed to Frank one-half undivided interest in the "J. (James) E. Moore Island Farm" with the provision that Frank would live on the farm and take possession on January 1, 1917. The terms of the agreement stipulated that Frank was to "...take possession of said farm on the 1st day of January, 1917, and live thereon, and it shall become his duty to supervise the entire farm by way of looking after the tenants that shall be cultivating crops on said farm and seeing to and keeping in repair the home place (and) all out-houses, fences etc....." For this, Hadley would pay him $25.00 per year.

Hadley was to furnish 12 cows and yearlings on January 1, 1917, which were to be raised and tended to on the farm and Frank would be given one-fourth of the increase from these animals. Frank was to provide two gilt sow pigs, and that all hogs raised on the farm would be mutually owned by Frank and Hadley with the exception of one sow and pigs, which would belong to Frank's wife Lizzie.

Some timber had already been cut and hauled to the loading dock which belonged to Hadley. Other timber had been cut but had not been moved off of the hills and out of the swamps. Frank could remove and sell this, with the stipulation that the first $68.00 from the sale of this timber went to Hadley. The

Moore Island Farm consisted of 750 acres of land more or less and another 120 acres more or less known as the Smith tract. Most of the property was swampland with the cleared land on some of the higher ground.

This agreement to oversee the farm operation lasted for ten years. On March 26, 1927, Frank and Lizzie signed a deed of trust to purchase the J.E. Moore Island Farm from Hadley and his wife Sallie H. Bunting for $4,000.00. He borrowed the money for this purchase from Z.V. Bunting. The deed of trust called for annual payments of $400.00 beginning on March 1, 1928 and continuing each year through 1937. The annual percentage rate on the loan was six percent. The deed of trust indicated the amount of land was 700 acres more or less.

Why Frank and Lizzie Barber decided to move into the Islands Section of Martin County is not known. Whatever the reason, they found a permanent home there.

The Islands Section was among the least desirable places to live in Martin County because of its isolation. It was off the beaten path, located on the north side of Highway 64 between Williamston and Jamesville. A loop road, nothing more than a dirt path cut through the swamps and ridges just wide enough for two mules or two oxen to pull a cart or wagon, connected Islands farms to Highway 64. The road meandered through swamps and over the ridges, past a few homes of blacks and whites who lived there. Dirt paths led from the loop road to the Holiday, Griffin, and Barber farms, and to the Upper Islands. Travelers to Williamston would take the west exit via Highway 64 and for a trip to Jamesville they would take the east exit. Sometimes the water was so high in the swamps that the best route to Williamston or Jamesville was by boat—from swamps or ditches to Devil's Gut and on to the Roanoke River which flowed by Williamston to the west and Jamesville to the east.

The Islands Section is only a very small part of the Roanoke River Basin, a vast tract of land stretching from the North Carolina-Virginia border along the Roanoke River to Albemarle Sound, an estuary of the Atlantic Ocean. Its swamps are filled with cypress, bold gum, and cottonwood trees and on the hills not cleared for farming stand pine, a variety of oaks, hickory, sweet gum, and sycamore trees. Beneath this canopy, wildlife is abundant. When the water overflows the banks of the Roanoke, the swamps and tributaries are filled, leaving only the high ground, from which the area gets its name Islands.

The Islands were a haven for the Indians, the first settlers in the area. From the cypress trees they made excellent canoes that were ideal for paddling through the swamps, as well as the ditches and rivers. A variety of game animals for eating and for making clothing and teepees was also abundant. Fish could be harvested from Devil's Gut, the swamps and the ditches year round. And the ridges were quite fertile for raising corn and other produce.

Which tribes lived in the Islands before the white man took over and what happened to them is debatable. Were they Tuscarora, Morotoc or Croatan? And when did they leave, and under what circumstances? And when did the white men move in? While there are no definite answers to these questions, there is no doubt Indians once called the Islands home, too.

This dilapidated farm home is typical of those farmers lived in from the 1920s to the 1950s. The only modern convenience that reached this Moore Farm home before its demise was electricity. Some of the rundown homes still dot the landscape in Eastern North Carolina.

Evidence found of their existence on the Moore and Smith Farms include arrowheads, pottery, and a few stones with indentations indicating they were used for grinding corn into meal. Indian tobacco, also called rabbit tobacco, still grows in the wild on the ridges, and Peggy Barber has transplanted some in her yard. Morotoc and Skewarkee Parks in Williamston and the Roanoke River are three of the better known Indian names that remind residents that the Indians once dwelled here.

At the north end of the Moore Farm was a parcel of land, about an acre in size, covered with underbrush and a good number of trees. The land around it was cleared and used for farming. We were led to believe this piece of land was an Indian graveyard, though I never saw any evidence to support it.

Occasionally, pieces of pottery and arrowheads can still be found in the fields after they have been plowed.

The Indians had long been gone when the first generation of Barbers moved there. In January 1917, the Barber family included Lula, who would turn 14 in April; Dennis, who would be 14 in February; Tillie, 13; Maggie, who would be 11 in April; Toby, 10; Effie, 6; Harry, 2; and Lizzie, age 1. In addition to these children were Arthur, 8; and Robert, 5, children born to Frank and Gertie Simpson, Lizzie's sister. In all, there were 10 children—five boys and five girls.

Before Lizzie died in May 1931 she gave birth to four more sons and one daughter and seven children still lived in the household: Robert, 19; Harry, 15; Ben and Major, twins, 12; Clyde, 10; Emily, 8; and Henry, 5. Lula, Dennis, Tillie, Maggie, Toby, Effie, and Arthur had left; Lizzie Margaret had died in 1919 at the age of four.

Maggie's sickness had placed additional financial burdens on the family. To pay the medical bills, Frank had to sell 100 acres of land in 1930. He had six more payments on the farm, money was scarce, and he was left with seven children that needed more than he could provide.

There was not much time for grieving over his losses. Frank desperately needed another wife, and soon.

How Frank met his third wife is unknown. Whether he pursued other potential mates in the community is also not known. But what is known is that he wasted no time in courting and persuading Icelene Davenport Bailey to marry him—just six months after Maggie's death.

The sun had indeed been shining on Frank Barber the day he married Icelene Davenport Bailey. Without her he may not have been a land owner after the depression.

Chapter 6 –
Surviving the Depression

The Barber family in the Islands was not affected by the stock market crash of 1929. They had no money in the bank and held no stock so it didn't bother them. However, the Great Depression that followed this economic blow to the American economy plagued the Barber clan like everyone else throughout the 1930s. The Great Depression turned Frank against the Republican Party and banks. His loss of faith in the banking system would cost him dearly later on.

The depression years were their toughest challenge economically. Frank had to sell 100 acres of the Moore Farm in March 1930 to W.W. Griffin, who was an adjoining land owner. This sale was necessary to pay mounting medical bills for Lizzie, who died on May 22, 1931, at the age of 49 of stomach cancer. This was the last time Frank sold any land.

His loan on the purchase of the Moore Farm called for annual payments of $400.00 through the year 1937, plus six percent interest. Dollars were hard to come by. Frank worked for a logging company felling trees from sunup to sundown for one dollar a day. Even if he had worked 365 days a year he would not have earned enough money to make the payment on the farm. The price for the tobacco crop, the main stay of the farmer in those days, dropped so low that one year Frank refused to sell his crop. What the market wanted to pay would not reimburse him for the cost of producing it. Instead of selling, he loaded the tobacco into his wagon, hauled it back to the farm and threw it into the first swamp he came to on his property.

But they survived, managed to pay off their debts and even acquire more land while many other farmers and businesses went under. He held three cards that kept the family afloat during that difficult time.

When Frank married his third wife Icelene he got more than a wife: she was a real work horse and at the age of 29 in the prime of her life. She was as bow legged as a cowboy, probably from carrying more than her share of the load from the time she was able to walk. Had her legs been straight she would have extended her five-foot, five-inch frame by at least three inches or more. Except when she was pregnant she never weighed more than 125 pounds and did not have an ounce of fat on her body. She could do anything on a farm. Mr. Buie Bailey knew Icelene when she lived in Bear Grass. He remembers the days in the 1920s when he saw Icelene plowing fields in the Bear Grass community, "working just like a man," he said. But when she moved into the Islands, she had more than enough work cooking, cleaning, washing, and caring for her kids and seven of Frank's children still living at home.

Like all farmers, they lived off the good earth which produced a bountiful harvest even during depressions. Taking care of the one-acre garden was mostly Icelene's responsibility once it was planted. It was a source of food year-round, either fresh out of the garden in season or, because she canned the produce for consumption, out of season. Anyone who has never picked, shelled, washed, and canned butter beans or other garden produce over a hot wood stove in a non air-conditioned home during the hottest part of summer in North Carolina cannot imagine how hard the labor is and how much energy it takes. Meat came from a variety of sources, but she was the one who always cleaned and prepared most of it. Hogs were the main staple because they were raised, killed, cured, and salted down for year-round consumption. She also took care of the chickens, from getting hens to set for chicks, to selecting one for dinner or supper, killing, cleaning, and cooking it. Herrings were caught in the spring and salted down for cooking year-round. Wild game such as turkey, deer, squirrel, rabbit, coon, possum, and turtle also were put on the table in the appropriate season. Fresh fish taken from gill nets or other means of fishing were often eaten as well. Also grown on the farm for eating were apples, peaches, plums, walnuts, pecans, peanuts, Irish potatoes, and sweet potatoes. Field corn was shucked, husked, shelled and taken to a local grist mill that turned it into corn meal for corn bread. Black strap molasses was raised and cooked for eating and for sale. Wild strawberries, briar berries, crab apples and grapes supplemented their diet when in season.

They purchased only the necessities, such as seasoning and flour. Flour came in sacks that Icelene turned into shirts for the boys to wear. Scraps from the table were fed to the dogs or hogs. Nothing was wasted and there were no junk yards—everything was used.

Prohibition, which started in 1920 and ended in 1933, also played a part in getting them through these hard times. This experiment to legislate morality was a complete failure, but it offered an illegal way for people who were struggling to survive to make some much needed income to pay bills. Frank paid some of his bills with money that came from the sale of moonshine.

Shortly before his death in August 1994, Robert—Frank and Gertie's second son—told of operating a 500-gallon liquor still for five years during the late 1920s and early 1930s. He said it cost about $1.00 a gallon to make the liquor, and they sold it for $3.00 a gallon.

Robert said they quit making liquor because he almost got caught by the revenuers. On the day the law enforcement officers almost caught him, Robert and his sister Effie's husband Harvey Perry were busy operating the still. Robert thought he heard something, looked up and saw three officers sneaking up on them. "I hollered to Harvey to let's get out of here and I took off! Harvey ran in a different direction and got caught in a wire fence about 75 yards from the still and was apprehended. I ran around in circles before entering a thicket of briars and vines. I could hear the officers falling down and cursing and calling me all kinds of names."

After his escape, Robert said he went to his brother Toby's home at the north end of the Moore Farm. Afraid the officers were still after him, he changed into some of Toby's clothes, which were way too big for him, and walked home.

Harvey was convicted of making liquor and sentenced to a year in prison. "I remember Effie (Harvey's wife) crying when the verdict was read."

While this episode ended this duty for Robert, it did not stop moonshine operations on the Barber farm. Moonshine stills were in operation well into the 1950s.

Robert said that Frank purchased a used Model A Ford with money made from the moonshine and that he would let Robert drive it, but not any of his other children. Robert said that did not set well with his older brothers.

Living in the Roanoke River Basin was an added blessing during the depression, though it also had its disadvantages. The constant rising and falling of the water in the river and swamps made it difficult to travel to and from town, as well as plant and harvest crops in the lowest areas, called bottoms, on the farm. However, there were advantages in that the Roanoke River and its tributary, Devil's Gut, provided a bountiful supply of herring, perch, and rock in the spring and bream and catfish at other times that could be eaten in those days without the worry of contamination. Hundreds of herring were scaled, cleaned and salted down in pork barrels for eating year-round. The river and swamplands also provided a haven for animals, both the kind for eating and those with fur such as mink, otter, and raccoon whose skins could be sold, adding extra money to the family budget.

Though the depression years were devastating to many, the Frank Barber family managed to use the resources available to the maximum and hang on to all but the 100 acres sold to Mr. Griffin. In addition, Frank and Icelene purchased the Smith place for $1,000.00 on November 15, 1935, right in the middle of the depression. The 50-acre farm included a home, barn and mule stable.

Frank and Icelene had four children during these lean years as well: Dallas, born April 19, 1933; Mary, May 25, 1935; Jasper, November 9, 1938; and Lester, May 16, 1940.

The four additions to the family brought the total number of children born to Frank and Lizzie, Lizze's sister Gertie, and Icelene to 22. Three of those children died at birth and one daughter died at the age of four.

While the Depression was pretty much over by 1940, Mother Nature would deliver one more blow to Frank and Icelene before they would see better times.

The flood of 1940 was devastating to farmers in the Roanoke River Basin. This photo shows the highest point on the Moore Farm. Once a farm home, the building was originally constructed with wooden pegs. It was the only building on the Moore Farm in which the water did not enter. Pictured from left are Ben Barber, Della Barber and her husband Toby, Frank Barber closing the door, and Major Barber. Ben and Major were twins.

This is a picture of Frank and Icelene Barber's home at the peak of the flood in August 1940. There appears to be a hat on the window sill at right. What appears to be baskets are placed on top of the Model A Ford from the 1930 era. The car was either a casualty of the Great Depression or the flood. It was one of the few toys the kids could play with that was not homemade.

Chapter 7 –
The Great Flood

While it had nothing to do with the depression, those who lived in the Roanoke River Basin would be delivered one last devastating blow before seeing better times in the 1940s and 1950s.

Nailed to the black walnut tree near the water pump in the front yard of Frank and Icelene's home was a piece of oval shaped metal with the inscription: "August 1940." Two nails, one on each side, held the small piece of metal to the tree. It was about three feet from the ground.

No one ever talked about the small piece of metal in the tree. If anyone wanted to know why it was there, they had to ask a member of the older generation. Those who lived through this natural disaster assumed that everyone knew what it meant, too.

In August, 1940, the Roanoke River overflowed its banks and reached the highest level in recorded history. The flood waters destroyed farm crops, livestock, and damaged businesses, and homes from Weldon, N.C., to Albemarle Sound below Plymouth.

Two family photos show the flood's devastation. One is a picture of Frank and his twin sons, Major and Ben, and son Toby and his wife Della. They are standing in front of the Glubber House, located on the highest hill on the Moore Farm. In front of them is a canoe, afloat in about a foot of water. That was the only building on the farm in which the water did not enter. The tops of the corn can be seen in the field behind the barn.

The other picture is of the family home. It shows part of a Model A Ford in front of the house with several baskets placed upside down on top of it. On one of the two window sills sits what appears to be a hat. About one foot below the hat is the water. The water was about a foot high throughout the first floor of the two-story clapboard farm house. Hogs were put in the upstairs of the farm house to save them.

Along with the metal tag nailed to the walnut tree, one other piece of evidence of the flood's devastation was bored into the floor of the Barber home. The wooden floor in the living room was covered with linoleum. One day someone leaned back in a chair and one of the legs pushed through the linoleum into a hole in the floor. That's when the children who were not old enough to remember the flood learned that holes, about one and a half inches in diameter, had been drilled in the floor to let water out of the house and to help in the drying process.

What caused the flood? For many years the children born to Frank and Icelene believed that it was a dam that broke somewhere around Roanoke Rapids, North Carolina. They would learn many years later that there were no dams on the river in 1940. The water flowed down the river naturally.

Lake Gaston begins at Kerr Dam, which was erected in 1953 for flood control. Below Lake Gaston is Roanoke Rapids Lake, a smaller lake formed in 1955 for hydroelectric power. The Gaston Dam was completed in 1963.

The water that flooded the Roanoke River basin came from the third hurricane to hit the eastern seaboard in 1940. The life of the Category I hurricane, unnamed back then, lasted 10 days, from

August 5-15, according to National Weather Service records. The hurricane entered from the Atlantic near the border of Georgia and South Carolina, moved across Georgia and up the western side of the state and crossed Tennessee into Kentucky, then turned and headed east into northwestern Virginia before dying in the Roanoke River Basin of North Carolina.

While there may have been other contributing factors, this storm delivered the knockout punch.

Except for one day, it rained every day in Williamston between August 4 and August 19, according to *The Enterprise*. The bulk of it, 3.07 inches, fell on August 15. Another 1.09 inches fell August 16. The total rainfall for this period was more than 8.2 inches. In itself, this was not a big deal because the river level in Williamston on August 4 was 8.1 feet. Flood stage, or water over the banks, was 10 feet. That level had dropped to five feet on August 14 when the Roanoke started its rapid rise, reaching a record 20.4 feet August 22 before it began receding. In the 24-hour period from August 19 to August 20, the river rose 5.5 feet or 2.75 inches per hour.

Although warned that a major flood was on its way, folks in Martin County did not believe it could be as bad as predicted and were not prepared for what occurred. A flood in January 1936 had led folks in the county to believe that a foot of flood water in Weldon, North Carolina, would equate to about one inch at the river in Williamston. In 1936 that was true; the water level in Weldon rose 46 feet and the river in Williamston rose to 14.7 feet, a rise of 42 inches, or four inches short of what was predicted.

During the flood of 1940, Weldon reported 58 feet of water and the folks in Martin County were expecting to receive about 58 inches, or about five feet. The river and swamp lands could easily handle this amount of water. However, instead of 58 inches, the Williamston area was hit with 125 inches, or 10.5 feet above flood stage.

The Roanoke River begins in southwestern Virginia, near Christiansburg, and flows through Roanoke, Virginia, to Danville which is named after the Dan River, the major tributary of the Roanoke, then into North Carolina near Roanoke Rapids. From there the river flows through Weldon and on out to the Albemarle Sound below Plymouth, North Carolina. The river is 380 miles long and is the largest of the seven river basins in North Carolina. Before it died, the hurricane emptied what water it had left into this river basin.

On the night of August 19 Coast Guardsmen from several stations, and boats from four North Carolina Coast Guard stations, began arriving in Williamston to assist in the evacuation of stranded citizens. Among the local citizens who helped lead the Coast Guardsmen to the many farms along the river was Walter Barnes, the husband of Tillie, Frank's third child.

One of the boats, carrying a reporter from *The Enterprise*, visited the Moore Farm. This account of the visit was taken from *The Enterprise* of August 20, 1940: "Farmer Frank Barber and a small boy were holding to their post over on Moore (Farm) Island at noon today, trying to save tobacco that had already been cured. He and the youth, sending the women and smaller children out earlier, were preparing a few eggs for dinner when members of the

Coast Guard carried their boats to the farm to make certain that human life was not in danger. Advised that the waters would not leave a dry spot on the islands, the old farmer looked out on more than a hundred acres of fine crops and turned his head to hide the tears that trickled down his face. There was a large quantity of corn in a barn. A dozen or more hogs and three hound dogs seemed to keep their eye on him as if they were looking to him for safety. Watermelons were floating."

Except for livestock that was moved to higher ground or put in the house and barns, and the tobacco that had been harvested, Frank and Icelene lost everything, as did the tenant farmers on their land. Times were tough, and the government did not reach out to offer any assistance. A headline in *The Enterprise* read: "Victims of Flood Eligible for Little Relief, Reports State."

The paper reported that 500 people were driven from their homes in Williamston and that damage in the county was estimated at $200 million dollars.

A four-mile section of the road from Williamston to Windsor which crosses the Roanoke and numerous swamps was damaged by the raging flood waters and closed for some two weeks while it was being repaired. An effort to build up the road with sand bags and dirt before the flood waters arrived failed.

As the younger children grew up, they never heard their parents talk about the flood or complain about their losses. It was not until many years later that they learned the extent of the damage and could comprehend just how devastating this was to those families who were still struggling from the effects of the Depression.

Frank and Icelene had borrowed money to plant the 1940 crop hoping that it would produce enough to pay their debts and have some left. Instead, the remainder of the tobacco crop had drowned, cotton, soybeans, corn and peanuts were rotting in the fields; the garden, too, was wiped out. Their dreams for a better year had drowned; they were floating down the Roanoke with the watermelons.

Chapter 8 –
World War II and Beyond

After the flood the topic of the day returned to the events taking place in Europe. Adolf Hitler and his Nazi Army were marching across Europe, but the American people were dead set against entering the war. When the Japanese attacked Pearl Harbor on December 7, 1941, the country had no choice but to enter the conflict.

The war did not negatively impact the Frank Barber family. In 1941, Frank had six sons between the ages of 15 and 42; none of them enlisted and none were drafted into the Army. The rationing of gasoline, tires, and sugar did not bother those who had no gasoline engines and who could raise their own sugar cane. And the Barbers who lived in the Islands fell into this category. The only gasoline engine on the farm at the time was an old Model A Ford that had been sitting idle in the front yard at least since the flood, a by-product of proceeds from illicit moonshine. To the last generation of Frank's children the old car was a toy, and a reminder that somewhere in the world there were people operating vehicles similar to this one.

In the long run, the war actually brought prosperity to the Islands. The demand for products to support the war effort created millions of jobs, and when people have money they spend it. The economic tide the war brought to the country reached even the people in the backwoods of the Islands.

During the 1940s the state began building dirt roads to the Islands farms. Moving from east to west, the first road built connected Highway 64 to farms owned by Millard Holliday and Will Griffin; the next stretch extended the road from the Griffin farm to the Smith Place and Anthony Perry farms. Then the road was extended from the Perry home to Highway 64 west, completing the loop road known today as West and East Islands Road. The final section of the roads in the Islands was completed in 1949 or 1950 from the Perry home to the Barber farm. To get the roads built from the Griffin Farm to the Barber and Perry farms, Frank gave land he owned to the state for the roadway and the fill dirt, and even cut the trees across Daffin Swamp to the Moore Farm. This was a monumental task because the entire three tenths of a mile stretch was swampland covered with trees, and all the trees and undergrowth was cut using shrub blades, axes and crosscut saws. Two acres of Barber land still bear the scars of these road building projects. The roads are paved today, and very few people are still alive who can remember that they were once cart paths.

As the roads were being built, other good things began to happen. The Barber family acquired their first refrigerator, operated on kerosene. Before this, the only ice the Barbers had was the natural kind from a winter freeze and occasionally in summer when a truck from the ice plant in Williamston delivered it in a huge block, enough to last only a couple of days in summer. The children learned that cold milk tasted much better than milk at room temperature.

The first gas-operated machine to arrive was a Maytag washing machine, complete with wringer. It was a godsend to Icelene, who had slaved all of her life over wash pots, wash tubs and scrub boards, wringing the water out of clothing and bed linen by hand. In winter she would get cracks in the skin on her hands that were so bad they would bleed.

Then the first tractor arrived, a Case, and then a Farmall. A good blacksmith, Frank made the first set of plows for the Farmall that were used to till the land. Tractors also were used to clear land and, in the early 1950s, Frank added a saw mill to the farm and the tractor was used to power it.

The final connection to the outside world was electricity. It arrived shortly after the final road was constructed.

Television played a part in getting the road extended to the Moore Farm. Frank was visiting his son Robert and family in Richmond, Virginia, in 1949 when he saw television for the first time and decided right away that he wanted one. Television did not operate off batteries like radios; they had to have electricity. When Frank returned home he learned that the electric company would not run lines to the farm because he did not have a state road to the farm. Frank got his daughter Mary, who was in the seventh grade, to write to W. Kerr Scott, newly elected governor of North Carolina, asking for his support in getting a road built to the Moore Farm. An engineer from the state department of roads contacted Frank and the road was soon built, electricity followed, and the Barbers got rid of their kerosene lamps and the boys no longer had to go to James Mendenhall's country store on Highway

64 to watch the Friday night fights on television—they had one in their own living room!

The roads also made it easier for relatives to visit; they could drive right to Frank's door regardless of how much water was in the swamps. Frank's brother Perlie would visit when he was drinking and sing and dance for him. His brother Clyde was a preacher, and when he visited he would read the Bible to him and pray for him. When Icelene's half-brother Simon, also a drinker, visited, he would sit in the kitchen where she was cooking and talk and cry. Salesmen even found their way back to the farm after the final road was built! The only creatures missing on the Moore Farm in 1956 were bears, and they must have discovered the roads, too, because they are now part of the wildlife population there!

Frank and Icelene expanded their farm and forest lands during the 1940s. They purchased the Swain Farm for $600.00 in 1943; the Bob Green tract of land in 1947 for $250.00; and the Nichols Farm for $1,000.00 in 1949. These land tracts are located at the north end of the Moore Farm.

Exactly how much land Frank owned is not known because the deeds gave the number of acres purchased in a tract as "more or less," and it was usually more rather than less. However, it was well over 1,000 acres, most of which was swampland.

The arrival of the tractor would reduce, and eventually, eliminate the need for tenant farmers. In the late 1940s, four of Frank's sons, Ben, Harry, Clyde, and Major, were tenant farmers on the land he owned. Three of these—Clyde, Harry, and Major—purchased their own farms in the early 1950s. Frank assisted all three in the purchases, either through loans or outright gifts.

For farmers who had been struggling to survive, the 1940s and 1950s were good times. Life on the farm was getting better, the number of farmers was decreasing, and the size of the farms was increasing. No one in the good old days of the 1950s could possibly imagine how much the tractor and modern machinery would revolutionize the farming community.

About this time a tradition of the Frank Barber family also came to an end. The annual family reunion, always held on the Fourth of July, ceased in the early 1950s.

Each year Frank would barbecue two pigs over an open pit dug in the ground. Other family members would bring desserts, corn bread, slaw, fried chicken, collards, and vegetables. It was a family feast that everyone enjoyed and a day when the whole family could come together. Every year a new crop of family members showed up.

Only one Barber family reunion has been held since those held by Frank and Icelene under those two huge pecan trees by their homestead on the Moore Farm, and that was at the National Guard Armory in Williamston, North Carolina, on November 26, 1978. And that was a reunion for all the descendents of Henry Barber.

After the reunions ceased, the only time families came together was for funerals, at which time many relatives met for the first time.

The last year that Frank farmed was 1956. There was only one child left in the household and he was not cut out to be a farmer. The land was rented to his children or grandchildren until his death in 1968 when his heirs took possession of it.

Chapter 9 –
Maggie

The hard times of the Depression were made a little tougher for Frank and Icelene when tragedy struck the family of Frank's daughter Maggie.

Tuesday, April 3, 1934, began much the same as many other spring days had for Maggie Barber Davenport. She was awakened around 5:30 a.m. by seven-month-old Elizabeth, who lay squalling in a home-made crib next to her bed. Liz was ready for a clean diaper and food.

Maggie forced her 26-year-old body out of bed to care for her only daughter. It was quite cool in the clapboard farm house, but not cold enough to build a fire in the wood heater. She would soon fire up the cook stove, and that would produce all the heat needed to warm the home.

The Davenports lived as far back in that part of the Upper Islands as people could travel by mule or any other means of transportation by land. The road ended at the Davenport home. The great swamps of the Roanoke River Basin surrounded the home and the farm. Flat bottom boats and canoes could be paddled from the swamps and ditches to the Roanoke River.

In the yard, chickens were coming off their roosts, and roosters were greeting the sunrise with their cock-a-doodle dos. Cardinals, catbirds, Carolina Wrens, sparrows, and mockingbirds were making their presence known in the nearby shade trees.

The sandy fields around the farm house were desolate looking, holding residue from the previous year's harvest and already producing a robust crop of new weeds and grasses. Not even the family garden had been touched since the fall. The 1934 farm year at the Davenport home, like their marriage, was in desperate need of attention.

Inside the home, light from the rising sun was beginning to peep in through the windows and cracks in the clapboards. Maggie, in a full length night gown she had made from flour sacks, sat in an old rocking chair breast-feeding Liz. Her bare feet were cold from the fresh morning air, but Maggie's mind was focused on more pressing matters in her life.

She was born in 1908, the third daughter and fifth child of Frank and Lizzie Barber. By the time she was 15, six more brothers and three more sisters had been born in the Barber family. Two of those siblings were half brothers, brought into the family through an illicit relationship between her daddy and her mother's sister, Aunt Gertie A. Simpson.

Like most children in the county during this era, Maggie's education was limited. Most of her learning came from observations of what she saw happening around her and the school of hard knocks.

As she sat rocking and feeding her sixth child, Maggie tried to think. Her past was not a place she wanted to visit, and yet it kept creeping into her mind like sap oozing from a cut on a sweet gum tree in the spring. And she could not see a future that offered much promise for a brighter day. She had only today.

Her short childhood had been somewhat happy, and she felt that her mother had loved her, but she was dead now. Maggie had developed earlier than most girls, and in her early teens was a free-spirited young lady that all the boys and older men looked at with a burning desire.

Despite warnings from her mom and older sisters, Maggie either allowed one of those to fulfill his desire, or she was raped. And at the age of 16, she gave birth to her first child, Herbert Barber, on November 14, 1924. Herbert's birth certificate listed J.W. Barnes, the husband of her sister, Tillie, as the father. However, more than one member of the community said it was not so, that Herbert was a child of incest. The true identity of Herbert's father would be buried with Maggie.

Maggie arose from the rocking chair, changed Elizabeth's diaper, and laid the child in her crib. "Got to fix breakfast," she told herself.

As she made her way to the kitchen, she wondered where her no account husband Joe Davenport was and what he was up to. Their marriage had not been a good one, but it had endured until Maggie had befriended Mack Knox over the objections of her jealous husband.

The census reports for 1920 and 1930 list only one Mack Knox living in Martin County. Mack Henry and Maggie F. Stogner Knox moved to the county sometime before 1920 from South Carolina. Maggie Knox died November 22, 1929, at the age of 34 from some type of heart condition. Listed on the 1930 census in the Knox household were six children: Ida Jane, Leroy, Elizabeth,

Mack Jr., James and Robert, ranging in ages from 16 to 4. Leroy would grow up and marry Maggie's sister, Emmy.

Without a wife, the 43-year-old Knox would be looking for a female companion. He found that companionship in Maggie. The two had three things in common: poverty, a house filled with kids, and little hope for a better tomorrow. Whatever Maggie thought of Knox, it had been her relationship with him that had caused much of the fighting between Joe and Maggie. It was rumored that Knox and Maggie had been having an affair and her husband suspected they still were.

Whether or not these rumors were true, the relationship between Maggie and Knox had strained the Davenport marriage to the breaking point. Violence had settled into the Davenport home.

In the first round that found its way into the courts, Maggie was accused of shooting Joe in the foot with a .22 caliber rifle. She was found guilty and sentenced to 30 days in jail by Judge Herbert O. Peele in recorder's court. The sentence was under appeal.

In January 1934, Joe Davenport had filed trespassing charges against Knox. Although the charge was later dropped, it let Knox know that he was no longer welcome at the Davenport home.

But that did not end the violence in the home. The same month, Maggie filed assault charges against her husband. It was alleged that he had hit her with a fire poker, causing her unspecified "bodily harm." In February, Joe filed assault charges against Maggie, claiming she had shot at him with a .22 caliber rifle while he was standing in the yard with his children nearby.

Although Knox was no longer welcome in the home, the after effects of his previous visits there lingered on, especially in the heart and mind of her husband.

As she knelt in front of the cook stove to clear the ashes and start the fire, she wondered why she had ever hitched her wagon to Joe Davenport. After Herbert's birth, she was an outcast in her own family and the community. She resented the community's condemnation. Perhaps she thought marriage would bring her respect.

Exactly how old Joe Davenport was can not be ascertained, but it was estimated that he was between 74 and 84 in 1934. He told a news reporter for *The Enterprise* that he was plowing in a field near Fort Branch (also known as Rainbow Branch) north of Williamston when the Yankees came up Roanoke River and fired a cannon shot that went over his head, scaring his mule and causing it to run wild. The Yankees came up the Roanoke in April and again in October 1862. Had he been 12 years of age at that time, he would have been 84 in 1934.

Very little information is known about Davenport. He married Alice Williams on September 22, 1886. The marriage register lists Joe's age as 21 and Alice's as 18 at the time of their marriage. Alice died October 24, 1923, of Bright's disease. Joe's obituary indicated that he had a son named J. Abron Davenport that most likely came from this marriage. What is known is that he was old enough to be Maggie's grandfather!

Striking a match to light the fire, Maggie knew it was not love that had brought them together. She and Joe were married in Williams Township on January 31, 1926, by Justice of the Peace

L. J. Hardison.   Eight years and five more kids later, she wished she knew what had driven her to marry such a man.

While cooking breakfast, Maggie roused her children from bed. There was Herbert, 9; Edward Francis, born December 26, 1928, and a spitting image of Joe; Dock Clifton, born May 22, 1930; and Gilbert Franklin, born November 18, 1931, whose black hair made him stand out among the former two whose heads were red. The baby Elizabeth was born August 26, 1933. Missing was her first daughter, Mary Elizabeth, born December 28, 1926, who died shortly after birth.

Their breakfast consisted of eggs, cornbread, molasses, and bacon. They washed it down with water.

After breakfast, Maggie gathered her kids and headed toward Colon and Nora Perry's. The Perry's were neighbors, farmers, too, who lived within hollering distance. She had promised to help Nora pop seed peanuts for planting.

As she walked with her children to the Perry home, Maggie felt like she was in a cage. The eyes of the community and many in her own family still looked down upon her. She was surrounded by poverty; unhappiness filled her life like the water in the swamps surrounding the Islands farms; and Maggie could not see any hands reaching out to offer assistance.   No matter which way she turned, she could not find a door through which she could escape from the misery that enveloped her very soul.

Popping peanuts is a boring job. You alternately sit and stand all day removing shells from peanuts. Put the peanut between the thumb and index finger of the left hand and pop the shell open to release the peanuts with the right, usually two peanuts to the hull. They used a tool called a peanut popper, a flat piece of thin wood about the length and width of a 12-inch ruler bent in a U shape. It was used to pop open the shell and protected the fingers from blisters.

Maggie enjoyed being with Nora; she was easy to talk to, an excellent cook, and a wonderful neighbor. They put their peanut popping operation on the front porch, where Maggie could keep her eyes on the children and enjoy the fresh spring air. Nora's children were working in the fields. There was no school on this day because of high water. It was a pleasant morning and it passed quickly.

After a dinner of collard greens, sweet potatoes, boiled ham, cornbread, and canned peaches, Maggie and Nora returned to the porch and were discussing a date when they could get together and make a quilt. In the yard, all the kids suddenly ran down the road to greet someone. It was Mack Knox.

Mack spent the remainder of the afternoon talking with Maggie and Nora and even popped a few peanuts while talking, mostly to Maggie, whose spirits he seemed to lift. Maggie could not say she did not want to see Mack, but his presence made her feel uneasy. He had been the cause of much strife between her and Joe, and Joe had warned her to stay away from him.

Nora was considerably older than Maggie and had seen her share of men like Knox. She could not see anything of value in him. He was good to look at, but so were some of her yard dogs. Though she said nothing to Maggie, she could not help but notice a resemblance between Knox and one of Maggie's children. She knew Knox was a taker. To Nora, he was like a cottonwood tree and its seed—not good for much of anything, but quite adept at regenerating itself far and wide wherever it found fertile ground.

Around five that afternoon, Maggie gathered up her kids and started home to prepare supper for her family.

Joe Davenport was standing beside the house waiting for her when she arrived. "I told you to stay away from Mack Knox," he hollered. Joe was pointing a 12-gauge pump gun at her. Maggie was standing a short distance from the house under a pecan tree, holding the baby in her left arm.

Joe accused Maggie of spending the day with Mack. Before she could explain her whereabouts for the day, Joe shot her and the baby. Maggie screamed, begged him not to shoot again, and put Elizabeth on the ground. Joe fired again, striking her in the head. She dropped to the ground. Maggie died instantly. Shot to death in cold blood.

The Perry family heard the shots and after learning what happened summoned the sheriff.

A reporter with *The Enterprise* gave this vivid account of what happened: "Davenport accused her of having been away with Knox, and the quarrel started.

"Davenport got his pump gun and claims that she started after him with a rifle. Holding the baby in her left arm, she started to raise the rifle and fire on him, the old man said. He lifted his gun and fired, a number of shot striking the woman in the abdomen and 52 others entering or piercing the seven-month-old child in the legs and left hand. The child was dropped to the ground by her mother, Davenport claiming that his life was again threatened when his wife started to raise the rifle and that he fired the second time. The lead bore into the woman's head, causing death almost instantly. Leaving the body in the yard a short distance from the house, Davenport picked up the child, entered the house and laid the tot on a bed. Said to have first considered suicide, the old codger changed his mind and decided to await the arrival of the sheriff. It is believed by some that Davenport has not yet realized the seriousness of his act, and that the suicide idea never entered his mind.

"Surrounded by high waters, the island was almost isolated and it was nearly three hours after the shooting before word reached officers and they could reach the scene. Out in the darkness a short distance from the humble abode the woman's body was found slumped on the ground. After removing the body into the house, the officers found the little child asleep, her legs pouring forth blood at nearly every beat of the heart. The other children, one of unusually low mentality, were either in bed or sitting around the room with the murderer.

"Stillness gripped the scene when the officers took the aged man into custody and an *Enterprise* reporter lifted the infant from her bed and started here (Williamston), leaving four little children at home alone with their dead mother and three neighbors. Other neighbors were asked to go to the home and look after the children.

"Riding in a wagon that was almost floated away by the high waters, the child never whimpered from the time she was removed from the bed until after she was given medical attention and placed in the hands of welfare workers. This morning (April 4), despite a fever of about 102, the little bit of humanity appeared bright at the home of Mr. and Mrs. Joe Cowen here. While the child has a ready appetite and is apparently holding her own, recovery is not certain."

In this same article, the reporter noted that Maggie had almost been killed when hit with a brick several years earlier by one of her brothers. The reporter added that Maggie had come to the newspaper office in Williamston seeking aid. "Each of the children was clean and fairly well dressed," the article stated. "Those acquainted with the surroundings in the home assured her they would do all they could to help her, but advised her that she would have to run Knox away first. She resented the advice."

Joe Davenport was jailed that night and charged with murder in the first degree. Maggie was buried the next afternoon in the Barber burial plot in Jamesville Township. Abe Corey conducted the last rites.

The Enterprise reporter covering the murder case visited Davenport in jail and described him this way: "The old man, reported to be about 84 years old, already has one foot in the grave, and his health is said to be failing him rapidly...apparently showing the effects of confinement and the resulting loneliness, (Joe) said the other day he was anxious for trial time, and while he still maintained that he felt justified in the tragic act, he did not appear greatly concerned over his fate."

Davenport told the reporter he was going on 85 years of age, and that he "had never been in any trouble before marrying into the (Barber) family." He told the reporter that only one of the Davenport children was his. Davenport explained that he had been born in western North Carolina and his family moved to

Martin County when he was five or six years old. He also said that all of his family records were destroyed in a fire.

At a probable cause hearing on April 12, 1934, Sheriff C.B. Roebuck said that Davenport had told him he planned to kill himself after murdering his wife, but did not have another shell. The defense offered no evidence.

The Enterprise gave this report of the trial: "Herbert Barber, nine years old, a student in the high first grade in the Jamesville school, and weighing hardly more than 35 pounds, was the only eye-witness to testify at the hearing. He said that he, his mother, Dock, Gilbert and 'Bossman' (Edward, his brother), and the baby had been to Colon Perry's shelling peanuts. Continuing, he said that Edward, his brother, went ahead with an unloaded rifle, that when they were nearly home, Davenport shot, striking the woman and her seven-month-old baby. His mother cried to Davenport not to shoot again, the boy said. She dropped the baby, and the second shot was fired, killing the woman. He said that Mack Knox was at the Perry home, but that he did not leave there with them. He said that the mother was holding the baby and did not have the rifle when she was shot, that 'Bossman' had the rifle and the rifle was not loaded.

"The evidence offered by Mrs. Dora Perry substantiated much of that told by the child, but she made it clear again and again that Mack Knox did not go home with the Davenports on this occasion. The meeting of the Davenport woman and Knox at the Perry home was accidental, or not at all intentional, Mrs. Perry explained. She heard the shots fired, and heard Davenport tell his wife that he had instructed her not to go to the Perry's. She did not go to the scene of the killing until summoned there several hours later by officers.

"Sheriff Roebuck described the wounds that proved fatal, and told of his visit to the Davenport home. The old man and the nine-year-old boy sitting around the fireplace were talking about the sheriff when the officer reached there. The other children, including the one that was wounded in the leg and hand by 60 or more shot, were in bed asleep."

The trial for Joe Davenport convened the morning of June 18, 1934, in the Martin County Superior Court with Judge Walter Small presiding. The defense pled guilty to a charge of second-degree murder and Judge Small sentenced Davenport to not less than 15 years and not more than 20 years in Central Prison at Raleigh, North Carolina. He was to be assigned to the state highway and public works commission.

Davenport died in a Raleigh hospital on January 26, 1940. He was buried in the Williams Cemetery in Williams Township. His obituary in *The Enterprise* indicated that he was believed to have come from Alabama and that he was previously married to Alice Williams. The paper stated that his survivors included only one son, J. Abron Davenport, and a small daughter, Elizabeth Davenport, both of Martin County. The paper listed his age at about 84. The 1930 census listed his age as 79, which if correct, would make him 89 in 1940. There was no mention of the marriage to Maggie or the other children born to him and Maggie.

Mack Knox's life also had a tragic ending. Maggie's older brother Toby found Mack dead in bed on March 10, 1937. He was 46. The death certificate noted that it was believed the cause of death was an overdose of alcohol. His occupation was listed as laborer. The death certificate did not list any next-of-kin nor did it identify the place in which he was found dead. Like the death of Maggie, no obituary was carried in the local paper on Mack Knox.

The violence in the Joe and Maggie Davenport family struck again on March 20, 1976, when their eldest son Edward, age 47, was killed in his home in Jamesville by Marvin Dail. Although jailed for the shooting, Judge Hallet S. Ward of Washington, North Carolina., ruled there was "no probable cause" and Dail was freed. It was reported that the shooting was in self-defense. All of Joe and Maggie's other children died of natural causes.

Herbert Barber, driving one of Dallas Barber's tractors, 1972

Chapter 10 –
In Praise of Herbert

Icelene Barber reared, or helped to rear, more than her fair share of children. She helped to care for her half-sister and three half-brothers. She finished raising five of the six children born to her first husband and his first wife and seven of the children born to her second husband Frank and his second wife and his wife's sister. She raised two daughters by her first husband and three sons and a daughter by Frank. Besides these, grandchildren flowed in and out of her life like the water in the swamps. From the age of five, when her mother married Thomas Gardner, until the night she died in bed with her grandson Marty Barber beside her, there was a child of her own or someone else's in her care. However, all of them eventually moved out of the house, except for one.

Herbert Barber was a midget-sized man that you dared not call a midget; he was a bastard when the world still was unkind to those born out of wedlock; he was illiterate; he watched as his mother was murdered by his jealous stepfather; he was separated from his half-brothers and half-sister. In the game of life, before he could even get to bat, he had been struck out by circumstances beyond his control.

He would most likely be a charge of the state today, but, in the 1930s, families took care of their kin or saw to it that they were adopted into other families.

Herbert was born November 14, 1924, the oldest son of Maggie Barber, who was born in 1908. After she gave birth to Herbert, she married Joe Davenport and had five children by him before he murdered her with a 12-gauge shotgun while she was holding her daughter, Elizabeth, and as Herbert stood nearby watching. His other half-brothers were Edward, Clifton, and Gilbert Davenport. Another half-sister died shortly after birth. Walter Barnes, who married Maggie's sister Tillie, was listed on Herbert's birth certificate as his father. However, some family members said this was not so, that Herbert was a child of incest. His size gives some credibility to this speculation.

The day his mother was buried, April 4, 1934, Herbert went to live with his grandfather Frank Barber and step-grandmother Icelene and a gang of aunts and uncles in that household. He was nine years old. Herbert always called his grandfather, "Grandpa".

Herbert attended school in Jamesville, but he didn't learn much. He could not read or write, not even his own name. He had no concept of money. You could give him a hundred dollars or a thousand dollars and he would not know the difference. It was just money to him. When he went to town and purchased something, he depended on the honesty of the sales clerks and shop owners for the price of an item and to return to him the correct amount of change. He could tell you what something cost after he purchased it, but not before. His way of expressing money values was different. Something that cost $1.50 was translated: "I paid 50 cents and a dollar for this."

Herbert was about four-feet tall and never weighed more than 80 pounds. In his own mind he was a much bigger person.

Perhaps that is why he loved to tell stories, because many of them were about him, stories in which he would often emerge as the hero. He never heard of Homer, but some of his tales were just about as adventurous.

Everyone who met Herbert got to hear a couple of his stories. He shared them with anyone who would listen. If the President had ever come to our house, he would not have gotten away without hearing at least one story from Herbert. It did not matter that you had heard the story before; he kept no records of who he had told them to, you would hear it again. In fact, you would want to hear it again to see what changes he had made to it since the last time you heard it! You never knew which facts in his stories were true, or if he had made up some or all of them. But his stories were usually good enough to make you think that some of the facts just might be true.

Herbert was a talker. You have to be to be a story teller. When he wasn't telling stories, he was talking about something or somebody. His talking didn't amount to much, but then most talk never does. It's not what we say in life that counts; it's what we do.

Nobody expected much from Herbert. I don't remember anyone telling Herbert that he did a good job or praising him for anything. That's sad, because he did so much good that deserved much praise.

Herbert was a good worker. He worked side-by-side with other family members. He chopped his share of grass and weeds from the tobacco, corn, peanuts, and soybean fields. He was there at harvest time, stacking peanuts, trucking tobacco, and gathering corn and picking peanuts. He was there when we put down wire fences in the rain and cold, shucked corn and fed the hogs, mules and cows. He pulled his end of a crosscut saw and split blocks of pine used to fire the cook stove. We sat by the same fire in winter to warm our bodies, and there I listened to many of his stories.

He took a great deal of pride in his work; he did not miss any weeds or grass when he was hoeing in the fields. When he got to the end of his row, he did not stand and wait for his fellow workers; he pitched right in and gave them a hand with theirs. He had a good reputation throughout the community for the amount and quality of his work.

We played marbles, hunted, fished and went to town together, while he was a man and I was just a boy. I spent more time with Herbert than I did my dad.

He didn't get any medals for it, no big thank you and no extra allowance, but Herbert saved my sister's life. One of my nephew's came into the house late one evening from a hunting trip. He was going to unload his 12-gauge shotgun in the living room, and had the barrel of the gun pointed directly at my sister Mary. Herbert, whose language always included a few curse words, used more than a few on this occasion to tell him to go outside to unload the gun. He obeyed.

A few seconds after he walked out the front door, the gun went off! The gun fired as he was unloading it, and he blew a hole into the wall of the bedroom off from the front porch, breaking a mirror in the dresser inside the room. My sister is alive today and has two daughters and several grandchildren and a great grandchild.

Herbert may have been little, but he had an ego as big as anyone else. Some of the boys were bragging one day about how much whiskey they could drink and still carry on. Herbert boasted that he could drink half a fifth of liquor and still stand on his feet. It was a foolish thing to do, but we all do foolish things sometimes. He won his bet, but it nearly killed him. He walked about a mile before passing out. It took him a week to recover.

For most of his life, Herbert stayed with his Grandpa. Occasionally, though, he would live with another family member. He once went to Norfolk, Virginia, and stayed for a while. When he returned he had many new stories to add to his list of adventures, and a photo of a big-busted woman standing in a bar holding Herbert, grinning from ear to ear, in her arms.

Herbert wanted his own home, and after begging Grandpa for years, he finally gave in and built Herbert a small home about 75 yards from our house down by The Barn. Herbert did not occupy his new home very much. He found that it was a lonely place that required extra work to maintain, and he soon moved back in with Grandpa.

Herbert remained with his Grandpa, caring for him in many ways, until the end. A few years after Grandpa died, Herbert moved to Williamston where he got an apartment in one of the government housing projects. It was the first time in his life that he had been on his own, with help from his Uncle Dallas and Aunt Peggy Barber.

Herbert loved the project. He found other people like himself, people who had few worldly possessions, and who pulled together to help each other. Herbert tended a small vegetable garden in the yard of his apartment and shared the produce with his neighbors. He could walk to the downtown area at will and find plenty of people to share his tall tales with.

Most of his neighbors were black, but that didn't matter to Herbert. Somewhere along the road of life he had turned Mr. Prejudice loose. He lived in complete harmony with his black neighbors; they were as fascinated with him as he was with them.

At that time and in that place, that was no small accomplishment for a white man. Herbert showed us, without ever giving us a lecture, how we are supposed to live in this world with those whose skin is a different color.

There's one other thing that Herbert accomplished. I don't believe he ever made an enemy. People may have gotten mad with him, but no one could stay mad with him for very long.

He died in Albemarle Villa in Williamston on December 8, 1988.

Little Herbert died never knowing that he was a much bigger man than he thought he was. I still miss him.

Chapter 11 –
A Thief in the Family

My first assignment in the Air Force, after completing basic military training at Lackland Air Force Base in San Antonio, Texas, was Dow Air Force Base in Bangor, Maine. To keep in touch with my hometown, I purchased a subscription to *The* Williamston *Enterprise*, my hometown paper, which is published each Tuesday and Thursday.

When I opened the edition of September 27, 1960, I was shocked to find on the front page a story about dad being robbed of $9,200.00, later revised to $9,800.00. It was one of the largest home robberies ever reported in the county, according to the investigating officers.

According to *The Enterprise* report, the robbers had parked their vehicle half a mile down the dirt road from the house. About 100 yards from the house, they removed their shoes, clearly leaving evidence of their unwelcome visit in the sandy soil. One of the robbers had large feet and the other had small feet. One of the burglars entered the home, with help from the other, through the kitchen window, and the one who entered the house apparently knew exactly where to look for the money. He lifted dad's trousers and, on their way back to their car, took the money and tossed the trousers into the nearby peanut field. Dad awoke around midnight and discovered that his pants were missing.

The story immediately brought back some haunting memories of another night in my parent's home when things were not so quiet.

I cannot remember the exact night, or even the year; I can only remember that night—a night separated from a thousand other nights by the fear that it brought to my innocent mind—and the weeks that followed. I know that I was just a very small and very scared boy, around nine years of age. The erase button I used many years ago to rid my mind of this night has not worked; it has remained etched in my memory. The news from my hometown paper had resurrected the events of that night from a file deep down in my memory bank.

That night I was asleep upstairs when I was suddenly awakened by loud noises coming from the living room downstairs. I could hear dad cursing mom, but I did not hear mom's voice. "I'm going to kill her," I heard my dad say. "You can't do that, grandpa." This voice belonged to Ed Davenport, a nephew who was trying to calm him down. Dad sounded like a wild man, moaning, crying and calling mom every dirty name he could think of. "Grandpa, leave the gun in the bedroom," Ed pleaded. Then I heard a loud crashing sound, like a piece of furniture had been broken or turned over. I heard the front door open and slam shut. Then I heard voices outside trailing off into the distance. I was afraid to get out of bed and go downstairs, so I lay there the remainder of the night wondering what had happened and why. Why would he want to kill mom? I asked myself.

Dad was a drinker, and when he got drunk there was no telling what he would do—you just stayed away from him. My older brothers told of times that he would come home drunk and beat every child he could get his hands on. They referred to these occasional tirades as "monkey fits," where he would rage like a wild man for two or three days and the whole family would scatter like a covey of quail to escape his wrath. To this day I can vividly recall the nail, the razor strap, and its place of prominence in the living room. You were whipped with the razor strap if he caught you doing something he disapproved of in the home. If you were working on the farm and he decided you needed a whipping for something he disapproved of he would cut himself one or two switches, and they were every bit as painful as the razor strap.

I got up early the next morning and went downstairs. The top drawer of the dresser that sat against the wall to my left as I exited the stairs looked like someone had hit it with a sledge hammer. Dad had turned his anger toward Ed when he tried to stop him from leaving the house with the gun, I learned later. He had lunged at Ed with the intent of hitting him with his fist, but Ed, being much faster, escaped, and the top drawer caught the blow. The furniture in the living room was strewn about and chairs were overturned. Neither mom nor dad was home. I don't remember seeing my two brothers and sister, although I know they were there, too.

I did not see mom for three days or know where she was. All I was told was that she was in hiding. I don't recall seeing dad either. I don't remember who took care of us or if anyone came in and helped us. When my mother finally returned home her left eye was black, and she may have had some other bruises on her body that I could not see. I cried when I saw her, relieved that she was still alive.

Nothing was said about what had happened. Then dad returned. The house was silent. There was sadness in the air. If ever there was any love between mom and dad it was gone. Things eventually returned to what seemed normal to us kids, and mom's black eye healed, but I don't think she ever healed on the inside.

I learned later that dad had hunted mom for three days with his shotgun, and knowing him I have no doubt that had he found her he would have murdered her. My brother Clyde finally persuaded dad to call off the hunt.

Money was the reason for the night's events. Some of dad's money was missing, and he had accused mom of stealing it. It was not until 1961 that I finally learned how much money was taken, and the name of the person who took the money for which mom was accused of stealing.

Mom was not a taker; she was a giver. She gave her heart and soul and every ounce of her energy to raising children, hers and dad's and a gang of grandchildren. She never asked dad for anything for herself. She would make butter and collect eggs, take them to town and sell them to get some spending money, but most of the time she used that money to buy groceries.

Her normal day started at 5 a.m. and ended at 11 p.m. And there were many days during the summer when she would be up at 3 a.m. and not get to bed until around midnight. She put three meals on the table every day; washed clothes and bed linen all by hand. I have seen her hands bleed in winter from the cracks that came from being out in the cold and washing clothing and linen, trying to squeeze the water out of them with her bare hands. She fed the chickens, milked the cow, made butter, took care of a huge garden; did all the canning, house cleaning, yard work and occasionally went into the fields to help dig potatoes and barn tobacco. Her light brown skin probably came from standing over a hot wood stove cooking and canning during the hot and humid summers, her only relief coming from what little breeze found its way through the screen door at the back of the house and the small window beside the stove. Whether she wore her best clothes or her everyday garments, she looked the same—poor—there was nothing extra in her life—just the bare necessities. Yes, mom was a giver. And those on the receiving end of her gifts still remember her kindness.

By the time I turned 16, mom and I had managed to save enough money to buy a used 1953 Chevrolet pick-up truck. It cost $500.00. She learned to drive that truck, no easy task for someone approaching her mid-fifties. She nearly stripped the gears learning to shift it, but she learned to drive it and it was hers when I left the farm to go into the Air Force. Mom got her license legally; dad bought his from a dishonest driver's license examiner in another county, a man he found through a grandson who had served time in prison for stealing.

Dad had not trusted banks since the stock market crash in 1929 that triggered the beginning of the Great Depression. That is why he had all that money in his wallet when the thieves came to visit him. These thieves knew what they were looking for and where to find it. Nothing else in the house was disturbed the night they came looking for his money, not even the dogs.

The two men who robbed dad were apprehended in Williamston in early January 1961. The leader of the duo was 22-year-old Roy Franklin Knox, dad's grandson by his daughter Emily and her husband Leroy, who lived in Portsmouth, Virginia. His accomplice was 22-year-old James M. Bowers, also of Portsmouth. They had already spent the money they had stolen from dad in September, wasting it on alcohol, women, traveling, and automobiles. They had come back for more, except this time they were planning to raid the safe at the Martin Supply Company in Williamston. Knox believed that dad sometimes kept some of his money in their safe. Knox and Bowers were preparing to make their move when a local citizen called police and reported seeing suspicious activity about a block behind Martin Supply. The Williamston police followed up on the tip and brought the suspects in for questioning. Bowers and Knox confessed not only to what they were planning to do that night but also to the robbery of dad.

Of the $9,800.00 stolen, all they had left was $164.00. Knox had $68.00 and Bowers had $96.00. As *The Enterprise* reported the story, the two had left Portsmouth September 23 with the intention of robbing service stations, cars and amusement centers. On their way south, Knox remembered his grandfather who, he told police, was sure to have a couple of thousand at least in cash. And he knew where it was, because he also admitted to police that he had stolen $500.00 several years earlier and his grandfather had never missed it. He would not have known about that, because he was not there when dad's wrath was directed toward his innocent wife whom he accused of stealing this money.

The two thieves admitted their guilt to the robbery in superior court in Williamston on March 21, 1961. Judge Walter J. Bone sentenced each of them to not less than 12 years and not more than 16 years in state prison. Both were sentenced on two counts: no less than six and no more than eight years for breaking and entering; and no less than six and no more than eight years for larceny. The sentences were to be served one after the other, not concurrently. Not one penny of the stolen money was ever repaid.

Frank Knox and I were about the same age. Sometimes he would spend a week with us on the farm during the summer, and I went to Portsmouth once and spent a few days with him and my sister Emily and her husband Leroy. In all the time I spent with Frankie, as he was called then, I never saw him steal or even suggest stealing anything.

Dad hated thieves. My nephew Herbert Barber told the story of his half brother Clifton Davenport who had taken a watermelon from a relative's field without first asking if he could have it. Dad found out about it and took the rind, tied it to a string, and made Clifton carry it around his neck until the rind rotted.

However, the picture *The Enterprise* painted of dad during and after the sentencing of Knox and Bowers showed a totally different person than the one who hunted my mother for three days with a shotgun when I was just a boy. The man who had stolen $9,800.00 was the same one who had stolen the money which dad had accused mom of taking.

These excerpts are from stories printed in *The Enterprise*: "Farmer Frank Barber could not hold back tears from his eyes when he told the wayward young man (Knox) good-bye in a courthouse corridor...."

Knox's wife Barbara and their three-year-old son were present that day also. "Knox called to his grandfather and said, 'I'm sorry.' Out of the goodness of his heart, the old man clasped the grandson's hand. Tears, welling up in his eyes, blocked any words the grandfather might have said under more favorable circumstances....

"Earlier in the day, the robbery victim volunteered compassion for the two young men, advising Solicitor Hubert E. May that he did not want to see them tried for their lives, that he hoped they would not get life imprisonment. Certainly, the old man's compassion helped pave the way for the extremely lenient sentences—twelve years in prison."

I never talked with mom about what happened that night long ago, so I don't know if dad ever apologized to her, or ever shed a tear over the misery he caused her and the children who witnessed it. And had Knox seen the misery he caused mom, he would have realized that the effects of that first robbery were far greater than the crime itself. Maybe he would have said "I'm sorry" to her, too.

Knox did not remain in prison for long. On June 15, 1961, less than three months after he was imprisoned, *The Enterprise* reported that Knox had escaped from a prison camp in the Raleigh area. However, he was later captured. Knox was released from prison on February 24, 1970, and Bowers was released January 9, 1969. Apparently Knox's sentence was extended because of his escape.

Whether due to the robbery or other circumstances, I have lost contact with Frank and his brothers Odell, Billy and James. I forgave Frankie long ago for robbing dad of his life savings, and I hope other family members have as well. They are still part of my family tree.

Chapter 12 –
Ben and His Bottle of Booze

Hindsight tells me we should not have pulled a prank like this on anyone, and especially my own brother. But entertainment on dad's farm in the late 1940s was mostly self-made, and when half a dozen kids put their minds to working they can come up with some ways to entertain themselves, and most of them will be evil. It comes naturally to kids, like a runny nose.

Ben came into the world on October 25, 1919, almost nineteen years before I was born. He and Major were twins, not that anyone could tell by their looks, or the few ways in which they were alike. Of the three sets of twins born to Frank and Lizzie Barber, Ben and Major were the only set that lived. Emily was born four years later, on April 21, 1923, but her twin sister died soon after birth. Just four months later Lizzie's third set of twins were stillborn.

Like all of my older half brothers and sisters, Ben's formal education was lacking. About all he could do was recognize his name when he saw it, and he could sign it.

In the 1920s and 1930s, the nation needed farmers, and farmers then did not need an education, only a strong back. Ben had a strong back. He would have been better off with a weak back and an education.

Ben left home before he turned 18, ill prepared for the world awaiting him. He married early and had two daughters and a son before his wife left him because of his drinking and abuse. He became one of dad's tenant farmers, a profession that pretty much assured him a life of poverty.

Ben magnified his problems, and his poverty, by drinking. He would rather have a drink than a meal, and he would hang around those who had a bottle until it was gone, or until they left with the bottle.

When he could get his hands on the money, Ben would also buy liquor, but he was very careful not to let his drinking buddies know about it. He was generous in some ways, but not with his bottle.

One year, around Christmas, Ben came to our house for a visit. Ben lived just down the road from us, and brought with him on this visit a fifth of Johnnie Walker. Our farm house was built on blocks of oak wood and was about two feet off the ground. Before entering the house, Ben hid his bottle behind one of the blocks of wood. The fifth was about two thirds full. The hiding place was a good one for adults, but for kids who were 10 and 11 years old, it was easy to spot while playing in the yard.

My brother, Lester, and I were entertaining four or five of our nephews that day. We were having a great time, playing cowboys and Indians. Our horses were tobacco sticks with a string tied to one end. We would put the stick between our legs, hold one end of it up with a string in our left hand and with our cap pistol in the right, we ran around the house hollering "Hi O Silver" or some other phrase used by the Lone Ranger and his sidekick Tonto. On these occasions, life on the farm was at its best for kids.

While playing this game, one of the kids noticed Ben's bottle under the house. We put aside our guns and horses and turned our attention to this brown bottle that had something in it. We opened it and it contained what we expected—whiskey.

We all took a little sip just to see how it tasted. It wasn't that good, so someone suggested that we pour it in the hog trough and watch the hogs drink it. And that's what we did. The hogs tasted of it but didn't care for it either. So most of the booze just went to waste in the hog trough.

I can't remember who suggested that we replace the contents of the bottle with urine and put it back in the exact same spot. We were operating as a team and didn't keep records of who suggested what. It took a couple of the boys to fill the bottle back to its previous level. We then cleaned the bottle and put old Johnnie in its original place under the house.

We were not too young to know that we were about to make one big brother unhappy, and we did not want to be close by when he discovered what had happened to that bottle. So we looked for a hiding place where we could observe the next step in this set up.

We chose an old tobacco barn, filled with bailed peanut hay, which was located about 100 yards from the house. From a small window in the top of the tobacco barn we could see the front of the house and the corner where Ben had hidden his bottle. We rearranged the hay in the barn so we could all sit back and see what would happen next.

It was a beautiful December day, sunny, very little breeze, and the temperature was around 55 degrees Fahrenheit. In the tobacco barn it was cozy, and the smell of fresh peanut hay made it a pleasant place to just sit and watch.

We did not have to wait long. About mid-afternoon Ben walked out of the house and stepped to the edge of the boxed-in front porch the family referred to as the "pizer," for piazza, an Italian word for porch or veranda. Before walking down the steps to the front yard, he looked around to see if there was anyone coming or going. There wasn't.

He walked down the steps and turned right and disappeared behind the house to get his bottle. Then he came back into our view and once again looked all round to see if anyone was coming. He was in the clear; he could take a drink and not have to share his bottle with anyone.

Hollywood could not have found a better position from which to film what happened next. From the tobacco barn window we watched intently as Ben opened the bottle. He held the bottle in his right hand, took the lid off with his left, and then stuck the top of the bottle in the inside of the elbow, pulled his left arm tight around the bottle, then pulled it out from the bottom of his shirt sleeve. Satisfied the top of the bottle was clean, Ben turned it to his mouth and took a swig.

His reaction was faster than a speeding bullet. His head came forward and out of his mouth came the urine. He stood there for a few seconds spitting and gagging, trying to get the taste from his mouth. Then he smelled the contents of the bottle. Now he knew for certain that it was not the Johnnie Walker that he had previously tasted from this same bottle.

Ben looked around. There was no one in sight that he could see. We boys were rolling in laughter on the hay in the tobacco barn. We had not anticipated that he would take a drink before smelling the contents.

We decided to remain in the barn for a while and avoid all contact with Ben.

It didn't work. Ben knew who the culprits were and he soon made his way to our hiding place.

"Which one of you boys took my liquor and pissed in the bottle?" he angrily demanded. Not having thought of what the consequences of our actions might be, we were all a little scared.

However, we assured him as best as we could that we had been playing in the barn and had no earthly idea what he was talking about.

I don't think he believed a word we said, and I suspect he knew we were all guilty.

I left the farm in 1957 and did not remember the incident until years later. I cannot think of the prank to this day without laughing. It didn't stop Ben from drinking, but I did notice afterwards that before he took a sip from a bottle he smelled the contents first.

Ben raised his three children the best he could, and when he inherited his share of dad's farm, he sold it and squandered the money. He lived in the old farm house that was on the land he sold until he became too ill to take care of himself. He spent his final days with his oldest daughter, Marie. Ben died of lung cancer on May 18, 1977, at the age of 57.

Chapter 13 –
Work, Food and Fun

Life on the family farm could best be described in three words: hard dirty work. Some jobs were more enjoyable than others, but work of some kind, like it or not, was waiting for you every day when the sun came up. And when you quit at the end of the day, you did not have to look hard to see more work that needed doing. Even on rainy days in summer and when snow or ice covered the fields in winter, there was plenty of work awaiting the farmer and his family.

Fun times were few and far between, so when they did come everyone made the most of them. Making homemade ice cream with a hand-cranked machine was work, but getting to eat some real ice cream afterwards made this an enjoyable thing to do.

Fishing was another thing we enjoyed doing, even though it was often labor intensive, too. For example, dad set gill nets in Devil's Gut, but to get to them we had to walk to the far end of the farm, and if the water was up, we continued by paddling a boat through the swamps to Devil's Gut, and if the water was low we had to walk. From our home to Devil's Gut, no matter how you got there, was a distance of nearly two miles. Then, we would paddle the boat up and down Devil's Gut to check the nets. That was work, especially when the water was high and the current was strong, but since it was something I really enjoyed doing it was pure pleasure to me. I enjoyed going with dad because it was fascinating to pull the nets from the water to see what was in them. It was almost like opening a Christmas present! Dad would remove the fish that were large enough to eat and toss everything else back in the water. Our catch would include carp, catfish, eels, white and yellow perch, bream, bass, blackfish, and occasionally a turtle. To dad it probably was just another job that needed doing because it put food on the table.

Catching herring during the spring run was another type of fishing that I enjoyed, even though it involved much work. Many times I have helped dad make a dip net, two bowed cypress poles with netting strung around them, and used it to catch herring when they exited Devil's Gut and entered Isaac Ditch. You can feel the fish bumping into the net, and it is exciting to see how many fish you can catch in a single dip. Again, cleaning the herring and salting them down in a pork barrel for eating during the summer and winter was a job. Another method used back then for catching fish was called the "fishing machine." A couple of my half brothers operated one on Devil's Gut in the spring of the year. A telephone-like pole was extended from the bank into the water where two flat bottom boats held the other end of the pole out of the water. Four paddles affixed to the end of the pole allowed the flowing water to power the machine. Two wire nets were mounted on the pole, one beside each boat. The wire nets were mounted on the pole so they would alternately enter and exit the water. As the paddles turned the pole, one net rose from the water and emptied its catch into the boat as the other entered the water. The nets were shaped so the fish would easily flow from them into the boat as they came out of the water.

Devil's Gut was a good place to fish. Black people who lived in the Islands would walk even greater distances from their homes across our land to fish in Devil's Gut when the water was down so they could fish from the bank with cane poles. And they always came back with fish in their buckets or on strings.

Mom loved to fish, too, and some of my fondest memories of her are the times we went fishing. I was home on leave the last time we fished together. She caught a huge catfish, one you could not sling into the boat without losing it. I grabbed the net and just as I slipped the net under the fish the hook came out of its mouth. But before I could get the fish in the boat, it flopped its way through the bottom of the net and back into Gardner Creek. The net had dry-rotted. You would have thought mom had lost her last dollar! She took her fishing seriously.

Another thing about mom and fishing is that she did not have any size limits on the fish she caught. You couldn't throw them back in because that would be like throwing your luck away, she would tell us. I have seen mom clean and fry fish that were so small you could use the whole fish for bait! "If they are big enough to bite my hook, they're big enough to eat," she said.

While it was rare that she got to catch them, mom cooked all the fish. Her fish stew was awesome. It didn't matter that the stew included such undesirable catches as carp, blackfish, or catfish. Her fish stew was a gourmet treat to us.

Mom did not mind sharing her recipes with anyone, but she did not leave any behind when she died. All of her recipes were in her head. She could write a little, but she did not bother putting her recipes on paper. Everything she cooked was from memory.

When I left home I was unaware that I would never again eat any meals as good as hers at anyone's table.

The two things that mom loved most in life were children and eating. It is a good thing she loved children, because she raised a gang of them. When she sat down to eat, there was either a child beside her or one in her lap that she was feeding and sometimes both.

One of her favorite foods was collard greens seasoned with pork that had been soaked in salt. I have seen her eat pure fat pork meat in the same way she ate her dessert. She enjoyed eating; she savored and enjoyed every morsel; it was a pleasure just to watch her consume a meal.

Mom cooked at least two and sometimes three meals a day, and there was never a time when the cupboard was empty. Even when we did not have a refrigerator, leftovers were kept in the cupboard—we called it a safe—and most of them would be eaten before they spoiled. My nephew Melvin Barber and his family lived a short distance north of us. Whenever his parents left the farm they had to take the road by our house. Before they would get to our house, Melvin would begin begging his mamma to stop at grandma's house to get a 'lasses and biscuit. Mom would punch a hole in the biscuit with her finger and fill it with molasses. He would happily go on his way eating that biscuit and molasses. It did not matter that his mother, Mildred, had given him a biscuit exactly like the one mom prepared for him; he had to have a 'lasses and biscuit from Grandma Icelene's cupboard.

Breakfast was a big meal down on the farm. Everyday we got homemade biscuits, ham and gravy, sausage or bacon; eggs cooked in a variety of ways; black strap molasses and Karo syrup. We washed it down with cow's milk in winter and throughout the year after we bought a kerosene-operated refrigerator or the strongest freshly perked Luzianne coffee with chicory I have ever had. While mom and dad and some of my siblings drank it straight or with cream and sugar, I had to water mine down considerably. Everything except spices, sugar, coffee, flour, and syrup was produced on the farm. During the hunting season, October 15 through December, our breakfast feast was supplemented with deerburgers, one of my all time favorite foods. Mom detested deer meat, but she knew how to cook it. I could eat her deerburgers any time day or night. They were best when eaten like a hamburger with mustard, the only difference being that I would put the deerburger between one of mom's biscuits and add some Karo syrup. Deerburgers were better than any hamburger I've ever had. It was rare that we ever had bologna or loaf bread for breakfast, but when we did we thought we were eating just like "rich" people.

For the noon meal, foods included fried or baked chicken or some type of pork, collards, cabbage, turnips and rutabagas to include roots and tops, usually cooked with pork. Vegetables included Irish potatoes, and, when in season, we had fresh green beans, cucumbers, tomatoes that were best when cut up and soaked in sugar with just a tad of vinegar, garden peas, butter beans, or field peas; for bread we had biscuits or cornbread cooked in a variety of ways. Sometimes we had fish stew for dinner and occasionally turtle soup. During the hunting season, meats may also have included squirrel, rabbit, coon, possum, turkey, and a variety of birds.

For supper, we sometimes had leftovers from dinner, but quite often we had another whole meal. Those meals included pork roasts or stews and pork chops; and a favorite meal of fried ham or sausage with chocolate and biscuits. I would learn that the latter delicacy was unheard of in other parts of the universe. Cocoa, sugar, and vanilla were mixed with canned milk and cooked in a frying pan until it was slightly thicker than a cup of hot chocolate. It was poured on a hot buttered biscuit and eaten along with the ham or sausage and washed down with milk or coffee. One other good thing about this meal was that a dessert afterwards was not needed! Many times I could smell the ham cooking while working at the barn some 75 yards from the house. Sometimes we would have sweet potatoes and sausage for supper, fresh fried fish or salt herring, fried cornbread or biscuits, and cantaloupe when in season. A treat I enjoyed for dinner or supper was clabber and biscuit with sugar spread over it. I also loved to eat briar berries, fox grapes, found high up in trees, other wild grapes, and mulberries. I loved maypops until I ate so many one year they constipated me. These little delicacies grew mostly in peanut fields and would ripen about the time we dug peanuts. They grow on a vine and are about the size and shape of a hen egg. Just pop them open and eat the seed and sweet gooey substance inside. I have eaten a few maypops since my bout with constipation, but they did not taste the same as before that unpleasant experience.

Drinks included cow's milk when we could get it and keep it from spoiling; iced tea when we could get ice; water, and Luzianne coffee three times a day. Cheese melted in a hot cup of sugared coffee was a real delicacy, too.

In season, desserts included plums, peaches, wild briar berries wrapped in flour dough, sweetened with sugar and baked in the oven; strawberries and biscuits, and pecan and sweet potato pies. Mom would make jams from pears, peaches, wild grapes and crab apples. Watermelons and cantaloupe also were considered desserts.

Mom also raised onions, radishes and hot peppers. In late summer and early fall, the hot pepper would turn red. Mom would pick the peppers, take a needle and thread and string them up in lengths of two to three feet and hang them behind the cook stove to dry. After drying, she would grind them up and use them to season the sausage when we killed hogs and also for seasoning other foods throughout the year.

One of our farm crops was peanuts which we ate year-round, and several pecan and walnut trees added to our food supply. The meal we used for cornbread came from the corn we grew. We would select the good ears from the barn, shell them, and clean all the chaff and other debris from it. We took the corn to a local grist mill for grinding into meal.

Other dishes we considered delicacies included molasses and hot cornbread, pickled pigs feet, cracklings and sweet potatoes, and on rare occasions oyster stew with soda crackers and lots of tomato ketchup. When it snowed, mom would make a snow cream that was almost as good as homemade ice cream. We would also get us a snowball and sit by the fire and eat it. Occasionally she bought a coconut, and we would share the juice and eat the meat like we would an apple.

We raised sugar cane and, in late summer, dad would get Mr. Isaac Nichols to come to the farm with his huge vat and turn the cane into molasses for a share of it. We would cut the cane and have it in place before Mr. Nichols arrived. My job was to hitch the mule to the press that turned the two iron rollers which squeezed the juice from the cane and into a wash tub. My job also was to feed the cane stalks between the two rollers and keep the mule moving to turn the rollers. It would take two or three days to squeeze the juice from the cane stalks and cook the juice until it turned into molasses. After Mr. Nichols got his share, there was plenty left for the family and some for marketing. We never got anyone other than Mr. Nichols to cook our molasses. An elderly gentleman, he was the best at this job in our community. I still have fond memories of Mr. Nicholas, a very pleasant and happy man, and the times we worked together to make molasses. One of the things I remember about sugar cane is that the raw juice is an excellent laxative!

Even better than the molasses was the honey that dad took from the two beehives behind our house. He would cover his body with thick clothing and his face with a net the bees could not penetrate. Even with all these precautions, still he would get stung a few times somewhere on his body. The honey was always good and the thing I remember most is eating the honeycomb. We all looked forward to the honey harvest because it was a welcome dessert no matter how you ate it.

We killed about a dozen hogs every year and would eat something from this one day's labor just about every day for the rest of the year. It was one of the days in which we worked the hardest on the farm every year. To keep the meat from spoiling, we always picked a cold day in winter to kill hogs. We were up at 3 a.m. and our day did not end until 9 or 10 that night. No school that day; the kids stayed home to help. Enough family and friends were invited to assist in getting the job done. Their pay for their labor was a gourmet meal and a few pounds of the goodies from the hog killing.

By the crack of light, hogs had been slaughtered and were being scalded in a huge vat of hot water to make removal of their hair easier. After the hair was scraped off, they were hung on a pole by their hind legs, gutted and thoroughly cleaned inside and out. They placed the hog on a table and cut it up into sections: feet, head, shoulders, hams, backbone, lean meat for sausage and fat for salt pork. Lard from the fat pork that was cooked was used to make biscuits and for cooking throughout the year. The hog skin was also cooked and the grease used for cooking; the skin, called pork rind, was eaten. Lean meat, to include some hams and shoulders, was ground up and turned into sausage. Parts of the intestines were removed, cleaned and used to stuff the sausage. We ate the hogs head to include the brains, tongue and ears; we pickled the feet and ate them, too. About the only parts of the hog not used for anything were the hair, hoofs, eye balls, and the insides minus the intestines used for stuffing sausage. No matter how fresh, you cannot buy anything on the market to match the taste of the food from a hog killing.

But it was work. Unless you have been there and done that, you cannot imagine the amount of work that goes into hog-killing day. It takes about three days to prepare for it. Mom had to do all the cooking before the big day except for the fresh meat that was usually taken from the backbone and made into a stew. Pots, pans, wash tubs, buckets, and tables had to be rounded up, cleaned and put in place. Firewood also had to be cut and dried and in place for heating water and cooking the grease from the skins and fat. Some items were borrowed from family or neighbors and had to be cleaned and returned afterwards. Axes and knives had to be cleaned and sharpened for cutting up the hogs. The smoke house, the sticks for hanging the sausage, paddles for stirring the lard and cracklings, and the barrels for meat storage also had to be cleaned. Hickory wood was cut in advance so it would be dry for smoking the hams and sausage. Salt and spices had to be purchased and in place. And months before all this, the hogs had to be selected, placed in a special pen and fattened. Dad would usually fatten twice as many hogs as we would kill, select those that were the right size on hog-killing day and sell the rest later. Our hogs usually weighed around 200 pounds. Prior to the early 1950s, all of this was accomplished with muscle power—from the cutting of the fire wood to extinguishing the last fire around the wash pot used to heat the water for the cleanup operations.

My earliest memory of a gas-powered machine on the farm was a tractor used to operate the peanut picker, which separates the peanuts from the hay. Dad did not own a tractor then, so we had to hire someone with a tractor and a picker to harvest our crop. In the early 1940s we plowed peanuts out of the ground with mules and shook the dirt out of them by hand or with a pitch fork. They were hauled to the center of the field and stacked around giant poles to dry. Sometimes there would be three or four stacks standing in the field, about 15 feet in diameter and 20 or 25 feet high. It took the peanuts a long time to dry in these large stacks so we later switched to smaller stacks, about seven feet high and three feet in diameter. There would be hundreds of these scattered all over the field. Two slats were nailed to the bottom of the pole to keep the peanuts from sitting on the ground. The year we began using the smaller stacks, a bus loaded with Germans—from the German prisoner of war camp in Williamston—came to the farm and helped with the digging operation. Two things I remember about the Germans: I could not understand a word they said; and they were hard working people. When it came time for picking the peanuts, a mule and a swing cart were used to pull the pole with the peanuts stacked around it out of the ground and hauled to the peanut picker. A mule was used to power the hay bailer. It must have been a boring job for the mule, which walked round and round, counter clockwise, all day long. Peanuts were picked from late October to mid-December; it was usually cold and no matter what your job, it was dirty back-breaking work.

Gathering corn was another task we did in the fall and early winter months. We never produced any bumper corn crops, but we always had an over abundance of cockleburs, which we referred to back then as sheet burs. These weeds were filled with the sticky burs, which would attach themselves to man and animal alike, and were difficult to remove. I've often wondered if the inventor of Velcro got the idea from this bur, because they also will cling to each other and are near impossible to separate. In dad's corn fields, you not only gathered corn but you were sure to gather some cockleburs, too. And unloading the corn from the cart or wagon was much easier than getting those cockleburs off the mule and yourself at the end of the day.

The money crop was tobacco, and it was this crop that drove me off the farm. I knew there had to be an easier way to make a living than producing tobacco. It was a year-round crop. Cut the wood for curing the product in December and January; clear a piece of land in January and February for seedlings; prepare the fields in March; transplant the tobacco in April; cultivate and add fertilizer in May and June; harvest in July, August and September; prepare for market in September and sell in October and November. No other job on the farm was as labor-intensive or as dirty as laboring in tobacco, and none more back-breaking. A new born baby does not require as much attention as a tobacco crop. Tobacco must be suckered, the top cut off; it has to be sprayed for worms and a variety of diseases; it must have just the right amount of water and fertilizer or it will not ripen properly; it normally requires the removal of three to five leaves every week, starting from the bottom and moving to the top, for six weeks, all during the hottest part of the year; it takes five to six days to completely cure a barn of tobacco, starting with 100-degree temperatures and slowing rising to around 190 degrees Fahrenheit. If the stems on the leaves are not completely dried in the curing process, it will cause the tobacco to rot when it is stored in a pack house. Tobacco requires a certain amount of moisture after it is cured or it will crumble like dried leaves when handled. The gum from tobacco, before and after it is cured, is difficult to remove from the hands. I used Clorox many times to wash it off my hands. The hardest days I have ever worked any where were the days in which I was in a tobacco barn at 3 a.m. removing tobacco that had just been cured, and then after breakfast going straight into the field and harvesting enough to fill that same barn before the end of the day. We did this regardless of weather conditions. Tobacco was tied in bunches to sticks about five feet long and hung on poles in a barn for curing. After the curing process, and before it could be put on the market, it had to be graded by color—bright yellow, green, brown, etc.—and tied into bunches. If we had been paid a decent wage for the labor it took to produce tobacco, we would have all been well off.

A job I thoroughly enjoyed was digging sweet potatoes. It was a back breaking job, but for some reason I always looked forward to November when we would plow up the sweet potatoes with a mule and throwing plow, finish digging them out of the dirt by hand or rake and place them in separate piles by their size, to include slips for use in making a bed for sprouts the next year.

Being out in the fresh air and sunshine in the fall of the year, scratching in the sandy soil and finding those beautiful Puerto Rican reds, made me feel good. You could eat these potatoes raw or cooked; either way they were good. After putting them in wooden baskets and marking each basket with a number to indicate their size, we would store them in the tobacco barn nearest the house. On nights when the temperature dropped below 40 degrees, we built a fire in the tobacco barn furnace to keep the potatoes from being damaged by the cold. The heat also hastened the curing process, making the potatoes much sweeter and juicier. Anything left in the field after we got what we wanted was picked up and fed to the hogs. We would sell some of the potatoes, give some away, and eat the rest during the winter and spring. The slips were used for bedding in April. Sprouts from these would be used to begin a new crop. In retrospect, the digging was the easy part; fixing the bed for the slips, pulling up potato sprouts, preparing the field, and setting the sprouts in rows by hand was back breaking. During the late spring and summer we had to plow them and chop out the weeds and grass.

Just about everything we ate came from the farm. When mom went to town to buy groceries, maybe three or four times a year, she only purchased items we could not get on the farm. These included salt, black pepper, a few other spices such as vanilla flavoring and nutmeg, flour which she bought in large sacks that, when emptied, were turned into shirts; sugar, coffee, Karo syrup, ketchup, mustard, and a few other miscellaneous items. Nothing was wasted; even the coffee and syrup cans were used for canning sausage.

Vegetables and fruits we canned included corn, string beans, butter beans, black eyed peas, beets, cucumbers (pickles), peaches, pears, and tomatoes.

Our one-acre garden was fenced in to keep farm animals out. It required a lot of work, mostly to keep the grass from taking control, but it was our favorite place on the farm. I can remember coming home from school in the afternoon and getting a cold biscuit from the kitchen cupboard and going into the garden and pulling up a fresh onion and eating them on the spot. Raw turnips also were a prized in-between-meal snack. We planted and harvested one crop of Irish potatoes in the spring and another in the fall. From the farm and that garden, we ate better than most rich folks, even though we thought we were dirt poor at the time.

As I grew older, I came to realize that the secret to never having to work is to find something you really enjoy doing.

Chapter 14 –
"Is This a Dry County?"

Getting off the farm to a place that offered some of the amenities of the times was no small chore for those who lived in the Islands in the 1930s and 1940s.

It was about a four-mile journey from my home on the Moore Farm to the country store owned and operated by Harry and Vonnie Reed on Highway 64, about mid-way between Williamston and Jamesville. Before I obtained a driver's license, I journeyed to that country store many times on foot and, later, on my Schwin bicycle.

Gasoline and oil, soft drinks, beer, an assortment of candy, ice cream, and canned and boxed grocery items could be purchased there seven days a week. The store also had a pool table. Attached to the east side of the store was a dance hall with a jukebox. Occasionally, local musicians would play for dances on Friday or Saturday nights. My brother Harry and nephews Louis and Hubert Barber were part of a band that played there occasionally.

Before I turned 16, most of my travels were to the school in Jamesville, an occasional visit to Williamston with mom and dad to purchase shoes and clothing, and to this country store, or the one across the street from it operated by James Mendenhall.

I could tell you more about places on my daddy's farm than I could about Jamesville and Williamston. Except for an occasional excursion to Hopewell, Virginia, my world was limited to within 10 miles of the family farm.

One summer night I was sitting on a bench in front of the store, drinking a Pepsi. A car with out-of-state license tags pulled up near the gas pumps. Two men got out and proceeded to enter the store. They both spoke to me, and I returned their greetings. Then, one of them asked me, "Is this a dry county?"

"Yes, sir! It shore is," I immediately replied in my southern drawl. "We have not had any rain here in almost a month." The man looked at me for a few seconds and then went into the store.

It was not until years later that I learned that he was not interested in how much rain we had gotten lately. I have laughed at that incident many times over the years, and it reminds me of just how small my world was when I was a kid.

Chapter 15 –
Farm Names

Just about everything on my parents farm had a name. Natural ditches that carried water from Devil's Gut into the swamps around our farm, the swamps and houses where people once lived, the mules and horses, and even the farms were given names.

The Dinner Bell – Not every farmer owned a dinner bell. The only dinner bell on the Moore Farm sat atop a pole about 15 feet in the air beside our house. Those working in the fields back then did not own a watch, so they listened for the sound of the bell to tell them it was noon and time to come out of the fields for dinner. And the mules knew what it meant, too! It could be heard for a mile away or more. As a boy I loved to ring the bell. It was used for only one other purpose: emergencies at the house such as a fire. I'm thankful we never had to use the bell for this reason.

The Glubber House – I guess the reason it was called the Glubber House is because a family by that name once lived there. It was used to store corn, tobacco, and bales of peanut hay. The house was nothing fancy, just a rectangular single-story home with an A frame roof covered with tin. It was constructed of clapboards, with the 2x4s visible from the inside. It must have been cold in winter and hot in summer, because it sat on the highest hill in the middle of the Moore Farm, and did not have a single shade tree. A 1940 photo of the house shows my dad and brothers standing in front of it. They were standing in water knee deep from the great flood of that year. The house was originally put together with wooden pegs, although it contained many nails from years of repair. My brother Arthur burned the old house and erected a small cottage in its place.

The Walter House – The only other old house on the farm used for storage was the Walter House. It was probably named for someone who lived there also. This was a two-story home that had a roof made of wooden shingles. Before its demise, it too was used for storing hay, tobacco and corn.

The Unnamed Home - There was one other old home located about as far back in the woods as you could get and stay on a hill. It was on a pine ridge that was part of the Nichols Place. All that was left of this home when I was a boy was the foundation and a few of the timbers from the roof, frame and flooring. Stones were used as part of the foundation. The trees and other undergrowth had pretty much reclaimed it. The road that passed this house led to the end of the pine ridge, then along a swamp, and just across that swamp was the Swain Landing Ridge, and next to it was Devil's Gut. I walked this route many times on the way to one of my favorite fishing holes. Whenever I passed this old house I would wander through it and try to imagine what life was like for the people who once called it their home.

The Barn – Located at the far end of the garden from our home—a distance of about 80 yards—was The Barn. The barn was constructed on wooden blocks with cypress logs from top to bottom. This was the only barn we had, so it was simply called The Barn. It was a two-story building used for storing corn on the bottom floor and peanut hay on the top floor. On each side and the back were shelters, and behind the shelters were hog pens and The Branch. About 40 yards from the barn were the mule and horse lot and stables.

One of my unforgettable moments at The Barn occurred one summer day when dad and I were preparing to hitch a team of mules and go into the fields and plow peanuts. We would always take a jug of water with us when we went into the fields. That morning something broke and dad was fixing it. He was working by the corner of the barn where he could lay his tools on a shelf that ran along the edge of the shelter. He placed the jug beside his right leg. I don't know exactly how long he stood there, but it only seemed like a few minutes when we began to smell something burning. He and I immediately started looking for the source of the smell. With my nose guiding me, I looked down and saw smoke coming from dad's right pant leg. The sun, shining through the jug of water onto his pants, had burned a hole in the leg of his overalls.

The Sawmill - In the early 1950s dad purchased a sawmill and placed it at the south end of the Swain Place where it was close to some of the best timber on the farm. Dad used the mill to saw timber for the construction of a building over the sawmill, which included a loft for storing peanut hay, and attached shelters for storing equipment and corn. The blade for cutting the timber was powered via a belt turned from a pulley on a Farmall tractor. This was the only building on the farm constructed from timber cut by this mill. Some boards were used for making gates, pens and shelters for animals, and for patching up other buildings. The building and the mill are still there but is not in use.

The Branch – The Branch was the name given the swamp that divided the southern part of the Moore Farm. It was more like a ditch with trees growing on both sides up to the farm land that was tillable. Before the dams were built on the Roanoke, the water that flowed down the river and into Albemarle Sound was constantly rising and falling. I can remember the water rising on many occasions and filling The Branch, and at its far end the water at times would run out into the edge of the field. As a boy I would place a stick at the edge of the water and come back a few hours or a day later to see if the water was rising or falling. The Branch was fenced in so hogs could roam there and eat the acorns and vegetation.

The Branch was perfect for hogs because they could easily make a wallowing hole for keeping cool in summer. One such hole contained a special type of clay-like dirt that we used to fill the cracks in logs of the tobacco barns. The dirt was mixed with water and mashed until it was like soft clay, then pressed into the cracks of the tobacco barns. When it dried it was hard and would usually stay for a number of years if left alone.

The same hole was a favorite of the mud daubers (we called them dirt daubers), too. They used it in summer to build their tunnel-shaped houses for the next generation of daubers.

Tennessee Branch – This branch was located at the opposite end of the Moore Farm from the one described above. It is not shaped like the State of Tennessee, and no one knows how it acquired this name.

The Well - We had a shallow well near the mule and horse stables for watering the animals. It never went dry and in the wet season the water table was only two or three feet from the surface and, at the driest of times, only five or six feet below ground level. In the summer, we would put a watermelon in the well to keep it cool and then eat it in the middle of the afternoon. This was the only open well on dad's land. All of the homes had hand pumps in their yards. The water table was always high; drive a pipe five or six feet into the ground and with a hand pump you could suck water out of the ground just about anywhere on the farm. There was only one natural spring on the Moore Farm, located in the woods beside the 18-acre cut, land on the northeast side of the farm nearest Devil's Gut. It was used only occasionally to quench one's thirst.

Names of Animals – I can't remember how many mules dad owned, but I do remember the names of some of them and one of the two horses he purchased when I was a boy. The mules were named Dinah, Kate, Kaiser, and Red, and one of the horses was named Frank.

Dinah – Each animal had a personality of its own. Dinah was blind and was a very gentle animal. I always had a soft spot in my heart for her. We used to tell anyone who didn't know she was blind that Dinah ate all the frogs she saw!

Kate - Kate was plain ornery, and stubborn, but was a good worker. I think she tried to drive me crazy. She would occasionally act like she was wild, but most of the time she just did little things that drove me mad. She would be pulling a tobacco truck and abruptly stop for no reason at all. Not expecting it, I would lose my balance and nearly fall off. At times she would take off without any warning, again causing me to lose my balance. Or she would knowingly take the wrong road. She was full of little annoying things like this, and I've often wondered if, deep down inside where I could not hear, she was snickering at me. You could whack her with a switch, but you did not get her to submit to anything. She seemed to have the knack for doing things she knew would irritate me. There were times when I wanted to shoot her.

Red - Red, probably named for her color, was an excellent worker that never gave us any trouble unless spooked. She was gentle most of the time but she could spot things in the hedgerow or woods that I never could see. Whatever it was she saw, if it spooked her she would take off running across the field, tearing up whatever crops we were plowing. I could ride her too, but I was always careful to get off whenever she started acting like she was seeing something I couldn't.

Kaiser - Dad got taken when he bought Kaiser. Because she was so wild, everybody avoided her, if possible, so she did not do her share of the work. She did not like to be hitched to anything.

One morning one of my brothers and a nephew were trying to hitch Kaiser to a cart. They got the saddle on her back, and she suddenly began kicking. She tossed the saddle off her back and kicked it into the air, striking it two times before it landed. The saddle is used to protect the back of the mule when hitched to a cart. The saddle was a piece of metal, usually iron, about two inches wide and a foot long with a curled ridge on each side, bent at a 45-degree angle. It was attached to two pieces of flat wood. This saddle was placed on the mule's back, and the chain connected to the two arms of the cart was placed over the back of the mule between the two ridges on the iron saddle. A rope or strap was tied to the two cart arms below the mule's stomach and tightened so the cart would not tip upwards when being loaded from the rear.

No one could ride Kaiser. One summer day while we were waiting for the rain to cease, my nephew Ed Davenport, who loved to brag about what he could do, began telling us about how good a cowboy he was. To listen to Ed, he could do anything. After he claimed he could ride any horse or mule in the county, dad not only challenged him to ride Kaiser, but offered him $100.00 if he did! That was a bundle of money then. Whether he wanted to or not, Ed had to accept the challenge. About mid-afternoon the rain stopped and the sun came out. There were a few puddles of water around and the ground was soaked from the rain.

Dad told one of the boys to go to the stables and bring Kaiser up to the house. We did not have any riding saddles, so Ed would have to ride her bareback, which he claimed he could do without any problem. Right there in front of the house, with everyone watching, Ed Davenport, with some assistance from dad, mounted Kaiser. He had to stay on her for 10 seconds. Ed stayed on that mule for maybe a second, two at the most, before Kaiser launched him heavenward and he landed on the wet sand next to a puddle of water flat on his back. Ed lay there for a while, getting re-oriented with the universe and getting his breath back. Without trying a second time, Ed was willing to admit there was one mule in Martin County that he could not ride. I would learn much later in life that people pay good money to see this kind of entertainment!

The Horse Named Frank - Somebody conned dad into buying two horses. He would never admit how much he paid for them or the circumstances under which he acquired them. He got the short end of the stick, however, even if the previous owner gave them to him! They were not worth the food they ate. Mamma named one of them Frank, after dad. I always got the impression mom named the horse after dad because they did about the same amount of work, which wasn't much. However, in defense of dad, he was too old to be doing much, but that was no excuse for the horses. I hitched Frank to a sliding truck one day with a 55-gallon barrel of water on it. I was going to take the water to one of the hog pens. Frank pulled it a few yards, reluctantly, and would not go any further. Put the switch to him and he would just lie down and refuse to move! So both horses remained in the lot and stayed fat.

Apparently there was a time when dad owned at least one horse that was worthy of its keep. My brother Arthur once told the story that dad owned a red horse that he would drive to town. Dad was a drinker, and Arthur said that when he had too much he could untie the horse, get into the cart, and tell the horse to take him home, and the horse would follow his order without any further guidance.

Praise to the Mule – The mule was without a doubt the hardest working creature on the farm. Dad had two steers, and I have seen them pull logs from the swamps and forest. But they could never perform like the mules. The mules worked throughout the year and especially in summer, the hottest time of year. They must have breathed a sigh of relief when they saw that old Farmall tractor doing the work they once did. The tractor eventually replaced all the mules and the horses. There should be a monument in every farm town dedicated to the mule. Without them people in this country would not have enjoyed such an abundant harvest.

The Mule Lot – The place where the mules and horses stayed when they were not working was called The Mule Lot. It was not a good place for these animals. At one end of the lot were two stables that provided some protection from the elements. A maximum of two animals could get into one of these stalls. On one side was an area with a roof over it where the animals were fed. A watering trough was at the other end and the rest of the rectangular lot was open. We cleaned the lot and stables each year in February and March, spreading the manure on farm land. It was good fertilizer. By the middle of summer, the manure had begun to pile up again. The lot was soggy most of the time, and with several animals romping around in it, the lot was a real eyesore. Whenever I went to the lot to get a mule or horse, I either had to wear boots or take off my shoes, roll up my pant legs, and wade into the wet manure, put a bridle on the animal, come out of the lot and wash my feet and legs. If it was in the summer, I would always take off my shoes rather than wear boots. Today, some animal rights group would probably put one in jail for having a place like that with animals in it. I do not remember any of our mules or horses getting sick or having any problems with their feet and legs from being in the lot. Nor did I. Maybe we were just lucky.

Farm Names and Place Names – Our farms also had names. Names were important in giving directions. Dad owned about 1,000 acres of land, bought over a period of 20 years or more from a number of people. There was the Smith Place, the Moore

Farm, Swain Place, Nichols Place, and the Isaac Field. I guess dad bought them from people who had these names. The Bob Greene Ridge was not a farm but a piece of woodland located at the north end of the Swain Place. The Isaac Field also was not a farm but mostly a wooded area with a couple of acres of cleared land seldom used for anything other than a pasture for hogs.

Numerous other places on dad's land were named, although I have forgotten some of them. Some of these include the Swain Landing Ridge, located next to Devil's Gut; Rattling Gut Ditch, which carried water from Devil's Gut into the swamps around the Nichols Field and Swain Place. Isaac Ditch was a water route from Devil's Gut to the swamps surrounding the Isaac Field. The Big Beasley and Little Beasley Places were small ridges near Devil's Gut; sometimes pregnant sows would go there to have pigs. After finding them, we would put the pigs in a sack and carry them on our backs to the farm. This was no small chore in winter when we had to wade across the swamp in water up to our crotch, with the sow swimming behind us that at times was not too happy with us running of with her piggies. Left on the ridges, the pigs would become wild.

Round Top Cypress was a huge tree with the top missing, thus its name. Hunters would often refer to it in describing where they had hunted or where they were going to hunt. Some swamps were also named: White Swamp, between dad's farm and Devil's Gut; Daffin Swamp, which separated the Moore Farm from the Smith Place; and the Upper Islands, which included part of dad's land but also extended well beyond it. Even one section of the Moore Farm had a name to match its size: the 18-acre cut.

Marking Animals – We did not name hogs or cattle, but they were identified with markings. On March 30, 1921, dad appeared before S.S. Brown, Register of Deeds Office, in Williamston to register the marks that he placed in the ears of "all kinds of livestock" that he owned.

Apparently this was required so that if someone stole your animals, you had proof they were yours through the registered mark on file in the courthouse.

According to the Records of Marks and Brands, Register of Deeds No. 1, Martin County, these were the marks that dad had recorded: Slit and under keel in the right ear and under square in the left ear.

As a boy I held the pigs for dad and my older brothers to mark them. I knew then that it was so owners could identify their livestock, but I did not know until December 2004 that these markings were registered in the courthouse.

Dog Names – Dad owned many dogs, but only two of them were given names. Princess was our only house dog, and she was purchased for my sister Mary. Jail Bait was a black, feisty puppy that was given its name because it was retrieved from beneath a warehouse in Williamston by Ed Davenport on the day that dad bailed him out of jail.

No Names – Chickens, ducks, goats, cattle, and hogs were not named. These were either raised for food, or to sell, or for both.

Chapter 16 –
Going Places

Getting in a hurry to go somewhere from the Islands didn't mean much. You could hurry all you wanted to, but it didn't get you to your destination much sooner than taking your good old time. The lack of roads and transportation kept folks in the slow lane until the early 1950s.

There were three methods of transportation: walking or running, riding in a mule and cart or two mules pulling a wagon, and by boat or canoe using a paddle or an outboard motor. Once you reached Highway 64, there was a fourth option: stand beside the highway and thumb a ride to town. Back then people could be trusted and most motorists did not mind giving a stranger a lift. But there were not many motorized vehicles using Highway 64. And if you had to pick up groceries or fertilizer, bumming a ride home was out of the question.

Just getting to and from school was sometimes the most exciting part of the day. In the early 1940s, only one dirt road suitable for driving a school bus connected the eastern part of the Islands to Highway 64. This stretch of road was less than a mile long and crossed Big Swamp and farm land, ending where two cart paths merged, one going to the Griffin and Barber farms and the other to the Holliday farm. This was where the bus picked up those who lived in the Islands section that attended the white schools in Jamesville. There were no blacks in this section of the Islands at the time; the black population was concentrated on the west side of the Islands, and they did not live as far back in the low lands as the whites. They attended schools in Williamston.

Getting to the bus stop was not always a walk in the park. It was not that far, really, the way the crow flies, but none of us could fly. We walked winding cart paths which took us around the Quarter, land that Will Griffin owned, across Daffin Swamp to the Smith Place, which belonged to my parents. From there we followed the cart paths around fields. The way we had to walk was a distance of about 2.5 miles to the bus stop and from the bus stop to Jamesville was another five miles. When the water filled the swamps, my older brother, Dallas, would paddle our sister, Mary, and me and our younger brother, Lester, across Daffin Swamp in a canoe to the Smith Place, or someone would transport us there in a mule and cart or a wagon. Many times I have seen the water so high the mule had to swim to cross the deepest part of the swamp. The Smith Place was on higher ground and, normally, the high water did not impede the journey from there to the bus stop. The road from the bus stop to Highway 64, when wet, was sometimes nearly impassable, especially where it crossed Big Swamp, and occasionally the school bus would get stuck in one of the miry spots in the road, delaying our arrival in Jamesville by as much as two hours. Sometimes the older boys would walk to the highway and thumb a ride to Jamesville rather than wait for the bus, which always seemed to run late. We attended school in all kinds of weather.

Occasionally, we would encounter snakes while walking to or from the bus stop. We once hit a snake with a stick and it broke in two pieces. We hit it again and it broke in two pieces again. We did that several times with the same results. It was the first and only glass snake I ever saw in the Islands. The next morning when we came by that spot the snake was gone. Someone told us that glass snakes would come back together, and I believed them until many years later when I learned that was not true. Apparently a bird or an animal had found the snake and eaten it. We found a Copperhead snake in the road on another occasion and I watched my nephew Gilbert Davenport stomp it to death. It was not a smart thing to do because it is a poisonous snake and one good bite could have put him in the hospital or possibly killed him.

In the late 1940s the state extended the dirt road from the bus stop to the Smith Place, reducing our walking distance to catch the bus to just over a mile. Shortly after this road was built, dad sold the timber on the farm and the company that purchased it made the first real improvements to the cart path from the Smith Place to the Moore Farm. The logging company placed two-inch-thick oak boards across the swamps so the log trucks could haul the timber out. The boards were nailed down so the high water would not wash them away. Automobiles were able to access the Moore Farm for the first time when the water was up so long as it did not reach the engine of the vehicle. Although dad had driven a Model A Ford to the farm and let it sit in the front yard and rust away many years earlier, as a young lad it was strange to see such vehicles being driven to and from the farm. Until this oak board road was built by the logging company across the swamps, quite often those who owned a vehicle and lived on the Moore Farm had to park their old jalopies at the Smith Place. Those who tried to make it across the swamps when the water was too high learned that vehicles can't swim, and the mules would have to pull them to higher ground.

My brother Dallas owned a Schwin bicycle. Sometimes he would let me sit on the cross bars and he would pedal me to and from the bus stop at the Smith Place. This was our first machine used for the hurry-up lifestyle. I remember riding with him and coming down the small hill from the Smith Place into Daffin Swamp and he would be pedaling at a fast pace. Those boards were less than two feet wide and some had cracks in them. In between the parallel planks was a space that dropped off three or four inches with occasional cross boards. Disaster awaited a fast moving biker with a passenger who ventured off the main boards. Many times I squeezed those handle bars for dear life as Dallas pedaled us at what seemed like breakneck speeds across that swamp.

Although we attended school in Jamesville, we did all of our shopping in Williamston where we also sold farm produce. Goods needed for farming were always purchased from Martin Supply Company. Mom would take butter and eggs and sometimes chickens to town and either sell or trade them for items we needed.

Shopping trips to Williamston were rare until the early 1950s when dad purchased a 1951 Chevy pick-up. Before that, shopping trips to Williamston were either in a cart, wagon, or boat. When the water was high, dad or one of his older sons would take mom to Williamston in a canoe or flat bottom boat powered by a Wizard outboard motor. They would go to the north end of the farm where the boats were tied to trees at the edge of the swamp. From the swamp they would follow a float road to Isaac Ditch, which entered Devil's Gut. They would motor up Devil's Gut into the Roanoke River and dock at the landing near the Highway 13 bridge in Williamston. They would walk from there to the downtown area, a distance of about three-quarters of a mile. The shopping trip consumed the best part of the day.

A trip to Williamston was a great adventure for this young boy in the 1940s. Dad raised some of the best watermelons in the county and in July when they were ripe he would take me with him to Williamston in a wagon loaded with melons. As we came into town, dad would begin hollering—almost singing— "Watermelons, watermelons, come and get a watermelon." His voice would carry quite a distance, and by the time the wagon approached the homes, those who wanted a watermelon were coming out to meet us. Dad didn't get much for the melons, fifty cents to a dollar depending on size. We always sold all of the melons. It was a long day, but it was just one of the many ways a farmer worked to make ends meet.

Riding to Williamston in a mule and cart during the winter was not quite as pleasant as the summer trips. Gloves were a luxury item we could not afford. I remember standing and holding onto the cart railing with one hand while the other was in my pocket for some warmth. Every few minutes I would change the position of my hands, but even so, they were numb well before we got home, along with my face. It took about 90 minutes by mule and cart to make the seven-mile trip to or from Williamston. The best thing about those trips was that we didn't have to wait for any traffic lights to change—there were none!

In 1949 dad went to Virginia to visit with his son Robert and his family. While there he saw television for the first time. When he returned home, he checked into getting one and learned that he had to have electricity for it to operate. Since there was no state road to the Moore Farm, the electric company would not run power lines to the farm.

Dad got my sister Mary to write Governor W. Kerr Scott a letter, asking him to build a road to the farm. The governor responded by sending engineers to discuss building the road with dad. To get the road built, dad gave the state the land, cut the right-of-way, and gave them the fill dirt to build the road above the water line in the swamps. The road was connected to the state road in front of Anthony Perry's home next to the west end of the Smith Place. Electricity followed the road to the farm and for the first time this section of the Islands was connected to the rest of the world by road and electricity. And the school bus could now drive to the south end of the Moore Farm, a five-minute walk from home.

I don't know how the mules felt, but that 1951 Chevy truck was a welcome addition to my lifestyle. I was also blessed to have a Schwin bike mom gave me on my 13th birthday. I would ride it to Vonnie Reed's combination dance hall, service station and country store or James Mendenhall's service station and country store on Highway 64 midway between Jamesville and Williamston. If I wanted to go to town, I would leave my bike at one of the stores and hitch a ride.

The state eventually extended the loop road east from the Smith Place to Grady Goddard's Number 90 Station on Highway

64. Mostly black families lived along this stretch of the road. This was a much shorter route to Williamston for those who lived on the Moore and Smith Farms. If one knows where to look, evidence of the old cart paths are still visible in some places. But few of the travelers today on the paved East and West Islands Road, or the Frank Barber Road, know about that time when life was lived at a much slower pace in the Islands.

Chapter 17 –
The Collision

I hope God has a videotape of my life, not that it's been all that exciting, but there's this one scene that I want to see from a spectator's point of view when I get to heaven.

It's been more than a half century since it happened, and while my memory is fading in many respects, this incident in my life has held up like a hot iron brand on a Texas steer. I've told the story to my sons, a number of times at their pleading, and I want to see for myself if it's as funny as they seem to think it is.

I was about 9 years old when this happened, and I can't for the life of me remember if I had freckles before or after this incident.

It was a cool, sunny, summer day in June, and I was sitting on the old wooden fence that surrounded the huge lot where dad kept the mules and horses. On this day, all the mules were in the fields with my brothers plowing crops. I was enjoying my freedom from school and looking at two pretty black horses and wondering why daddy kept them because they were fat and useless; no one could get them to do anything. If I, or one of my brothers, had been that lazy daddy would have killed us on the spot!

Suddenly, my thoughts were interrupted by a call from my mom: "Jas...per!" she yelled. When you shout a name like that it seems to carry much farther than a name like John or Bill. Mom was at the house, about 75 yards away, and it sounded like she was standing behind me.

Only the Lord knows why, but on this occasion I responded to the call just like a light bulb when you hit the switch. Why I responded so quickly is a mystery to me to this day, because normally if she could not see me there was no need to call—because I wasn't coming!

But on this day I jumped off that fence and hit the ground running in my bare feet. When I hit the sandy path that took me around the tobacco barn I could feel sand in my toes as they tossed it into the air behind me.

When I rounded the bend, the tobacco barn was to my left and the house was in front of me, and I was wide open! I felt like I could fly if I just put my arms out. Nothing could catch me! As I rounded the curve, I thought I glimpsed something chasing me out of the corner of my right eye. Still running at full speed, I turned my head to see if there really was anything chasing me.

There was nothing behind me, but when I turned around there was something in front of me: a huge pecan tree. What I saw at that split second I distinctly remember: the rough gray bark, the ridges that ran up and down the trunk, and the holes the woodpeckers had drilled into it looking for bugs. At that distance, the holes were much bigger than I had ever imagined. It was too late for me to turn left or right or to put on the brakes; in fact I didn't even have time to think about stopping. I hit that tree dead center and didn't even cause a leaf on it to move. I bounced back like a basketball with the air let out of it.

The impact must have knocked me out for a few seconds, because I remember looking up at all those stars that seemed so much closer to earth in a blue sky, and all I could think of was what people would think if they found out I had run into that tree, in the middle of the day, in the middle of a 100-acre farm!

I was blessed that day; I didn't kill myself, and almost as importantly, no one saw me! And I didn't say a word about it until many years later when I shared the incident with my sons.

Yes, Lord, that's the scene I want to review of my life. I want to see if that really was me that ran into that tree, or if I was just dreaming. And I still don't see it as being funny.

That pecan tree is still standing, and I recently had the opportunity to inspect it again, to see if there might be a slight indentation where I struck it. There wasn't. As I walked slowly past it, I wondered what the tree would say if it could talk to me. Probably something like, "Have you run into any trees lately, boy?"

I thought I heard a little chuckle as I walked beneath its branches, but, this time, I didn't look back. I just got into my pick up truck and went home; just thinking about this experience had given me a headache.

Chapter 18 –
Escaping the Jaws of Death

If I were a cat, I would have used up my nine lives long ago. The times that I have escaped the jaws of death are too numerous to mention. I believe with all my heart that the reason I am not six feet under the earth today is because God has been looking out for this country boy.

It began when I was quite young: paddling through the swamps in a hog trough or in one of mom's wash tubs when I could not swim a lick; shooting myself with a .22 caliber rifle—the bullet entering my body between my testicles and lodging near my appendix; running through snake-infested swamps barefoot; and falling off a land plaster spreader between the legs of a mule that spooked and flipped the spreader over her head without stomping me to death. Such little escapades made life more exhilarating than I would have liked.

Some of these events happened so quickly I did not have time to get scared; however, that was not the case when I had to ride anywhere with dad driving his 1955 Chevy. God knew exactly where I was when I was riding with him, because I was talking to him the whole time!

An honest driver's license examiner would never have approved of dad getting a license. And to my knowledge dad never went to get a license from an honest one, either! One of dad's grandson's, who had been in prison, put him in touch with a dishonest examiner. And a driver's license from a dishonest examiner is exactly the same as one from an honest examiner.

In the late 1920s dad owned a Model A Ford, and he was no doubt a good driver then. But in 1955 he was 77 years old and his brand new 1955 Chevy was like a space ship compared to that Model A Ford. With the proper training he probably could have gotten a license legally. But he didn't get any training and he did not know about the rules of the road.

The words I most hated to hear after he got that car were: "Come on, boy! We're going to town." I don't ever remember riding with him when I didn't pray—constantly. I don't think he knew if he was driving 40 mph or 95 mph. I'm not even sure he knew the difference between the speedometer and the gasoline gauge!

I was not the only passenger who wanted to stay at home. My nephew Herbert Barber rode with him to Jamesville one night. On the way back, an approaching driver did not dim the headlights. Herbert said, "Grandpa put on his bright lights and pulled over into the other lane. The other car dimmed those lights then!" I don't think that maneuver is in the driver's manual, but it worked for dad!

My brother Arthur was visiting with us and dad asked him to ride to Jamesville with him one night. I suspect they went to visit the ABC store in Jamesville. Arthur had not ridden with him before. About a half-hour after they departed, dad returned but without Arthur. When I asked dad what happened to Arthur, he said Arthur did not approve of his driving so he put him out at Gardner Creek. Arthur had to get someone to bring him home.

Dad loved to drive the car around the farm, and quite often we would see him walking back to the house. The car would be stuck in one of the fields and we would have to go pull him out with the tractor.

God must have been watching out for dad, too, because he did not kill himself or anyone else before he finally decided to leave the driving to someone else.

Chapter 19 –
Nellie

I do not remember my dad ever buying a dog, but we had dogs. Except for two of them, I have no recollection of where they came from.

Mom purchased Princess for my sister Mary. The other dog, a black, mixed-breed puppy, was retrieved from beneath a tobacco warehouse in Williamston, North Carolina. Dad had gone to town to bail his grandson, Ed Davenport, out of jail. Ed spotted the dog under the warehouse. It was whining and looked like it had not been fed in days. Ed crawled under the warehouse and caught the dog and brought it to our house. Some thought it appropriate to name the mutt Jail Bait. When Ed left home, the dog stayed with us. Princess was a good house pet, and Jail Bait was a good hunting dog. Those two animals were the cream of the crop of the hoard of dogs that took up residence at our home.

I had heard the expression "raining cats and dogs," but I never saw any of either arrive at our house via the rain. I can only speculate that the stray dogs that took up residence at our house had been deemed useless for anything other than barking and eating and their owners had released them in the Islands Section of Martin County where we lived to get rid of them. Smart dogs may have found their way home, but these dogs were lacking smarts.

Only Princess and Jail Bait were given names. All the others were just called dogs. To say they were completely useless would not be fair to them. When we castrated pigs, gutted rabbits and squirrels, killed hogs, or cleaned fish, they were always around to clean up the residue from the cleaning operation. They were four-legged buzzards!

Looking back, it has occurred to me that none of the dogs went to the homes of my three brothers who also lived on the farm.

Dad did not believe in killing anything unless you ate it. These animals must have known that we did not eat dogs. As long as the dogs did not keep dad awake at night or kill any of the farm animals, they could live in peace at our house. Violate those two rules and dad would convert them into food for the two-legged buzzards! My brothers did not eat dogs either, but they were not as kind to dogs that did not earn their keep.

This exposure to the doggie kingdom had left me with the feeling that I did not want one of these creatures as my best friend.

But then, at the age of 14, I became acquainted with Nellie. She was a German shepherd. Her hair was mostly blonde with a slight mixture of black on her back and ears. I don't know if Nellie was 100 percent German shepherd, but if she wasn't, she must have been as close as she could get without being a pure breed.

My brother, Harry, who lived about half a mile down the dirt road from our house, acquired Nellie when she was a puppy. Back then, poor families did not purchase dogs, so he probably made some other dog owner happy by taking a female off his hands. She was a good dog with the children. But wherever Harry went, Nellie went with him. Dad assisted Harry in the purchase of a farm on Highway 64 before Nellie reached adulthood, and I did not see the dog much after they moved to their new home. At the time I was just thankful that Nellie did not join the pack of mongrels at our house.

A couple of years later, I was visiting with Harry one Sunday afternoon. Harry and I were sitting on the front porch discussing the weather and the new crops that were off to a good start. Nellie was lying on the porch staying cool. In addition to farming, Harry raised hogs. The fences that kept the animals from getting into the fields were not that difficult to overcome for a sow that was looking for greener pastures.

As we sat talking, Harry noticed that one of his sows had jumped the fence and was eating the top off of the corn that was about eight inches high in a field about 200 yards from his house. I thought to myself, "Looks like I'm going to be helping chase hogs this afternoon."

But it was not to be. Harry didn't even get out of his chair. He just hollered, "Nellie," and pointing toward the hog in the field, said, "go get'em."

The dog jumped up and took off through the family garden, jumped a drainage ditch and sailed toward the sow, which must have thought she was in "hog heaven" in that corn field. She was about to discover it was not that at all!

I stood up so I could get a good view. Nellie never barked and ran so swiftly that she caught the sow by surprise. She began nipping it in the butt, and it was not long before that hog found her way back into the fenced wooded area from whence she had come. Once the hog was in the pasture, Nellie returned to the porch, panting heavily.

Harry patted the dog before it lay down and gave it some well earned "attaboys." After giving Nellie time to recover from her afternoon chore, Harry and I went down to the pasture and repaired the fence. Nellie went too, but never bothered the hogs. We saw the sow that had jumped over the fence. She was a little bloody on the rear from the nipping, but otherwise was okay.

That was the first time a dog had really impressed me.

The next time I saw Nellie was in Williamston. She was in the back of Harry's pick-up truck, which was parked just off Washington Street near the front entrance to Martin Supply. I learned that day that Harry did not have to lock the doors to his truck or worry about anyone taking anything from the cab or the bed of his truck. Nellie sat in the back of the truck like a soldier on guard duty. She did not bother people who were constantly going and coming on the sidewalk, but nobody better mess with Harry's pick up unless he was there.

I was impressed again. Yeah, I'd like to have a friend like that.

A few weeks later, I learned something else amazing about Nellie. Junior Jones, Louis Barber and a few other musicians often came to Harry's place on Saturday night to play music. No, Nellie didn't play or sing in the band, but she did guard the yard.

About 11 p.m. one Saturday night, we heard someone hollering to Harry. It was our brother, Dick, who was drunk again. Nellie was in the yard growling, and Dick was standing between the ditch and Highway 64. Nellie did not allow drunks in the yard unless Harry or his wife, Kathleen, both teetotalers, called off the dog. Harry assured me that he did not train the dog to stop drunks from coming into the yard, but he never stopped Nellie from doing it either.

That winter, Harry invited me to go squirrel hunting with him. He had bragged about how Nellie could tree squirrels and never bark. That I had to see to believe. All the dogs I had ever seen barked when they treed a squirrel. I had asked myself, "How can you find a dog that doesn't bark?"

One cold but sunny day between Christmas and New Year's, Harry dropped by the house to see if I could go hunting with him and Nellie. Dad agreed to let me go.

After lunch, we headed out. We started at the far end of dad's farm, and followed a swamp, which was unusually dry. We walked along the edge of the swamp so the dog could hunt both the ridge and the swamp. As soon as we entered the woods, Nellie disappeared.

Harry stopped near the swamp. After we had waited a few minutes, I asked him what we were waiting for. "For the dog to tree a squirrel," he replied. About that time Nellie showed up. "She's treed one," said Harry. We followed the dog. About 100 yards from where we had been standing, Nellie led us to a white oak, sat down and looked up into the tree. She had not made a single sound, other than the noise from walking on the dry leaves.

Harry had his .22 caliber semi-automatic Winchester rifle and I was carrying a 12-gauge semi-automatic Browning shotgun. If the squirrel stayed put, Harry would shoot it; if it made a run for it, I would do the shooting. But first we had to find out if there really was a squirrel up that tree.

Harry found a spot where he could get a good view of the whole tree. Then he told me to slowly walk to the other side of the tree. As I passed the trunk of the tree, he told me to stop. Then I heard the crack of his .22, and the "whop" sound that followed, which told me a squirrel was about to fall from the tree. "Well," I told myself, "that was pretty good."

Then we walked across the swamp and stopped at the end of a ridge covered with pine, oak and sweet gum. Nellie had disappeared again, and we were standing on the ridge enjoying the beauty of the forest and waiting for Nellie to return. She did, and just like before, she led us to a bold gum in the middle of the almost bone dry swamp. Nellie repeated her previous performance, and we went through the same routine again. This time I made it all the way to the other side of the tree and turned around to begin my search for the squirrel. I didn't see anything. Then Harry asked me to make some noise. This I did by shaking one of the smaller trees and rustling the leaves under my feet. Harry hollered, "Whoa!" I looked up the tree but still saw nothing. Harry squeezed the trigger on his .22 again, and another squirrel came tumbling down.

"Boy, that's some dog," I said to myself.

I picked up the squirrel and took it to Harry. "There's another squirrel up that tree," Harry said. I looked for the dog. She had moved to a different location, but she was still looking up that same bold gum tree.

"Wow! A dog that can count, too," I said to myself.

I walked to the other side of the bold gum while Harry repositioned himself. We searched the tree for several minutes, with me making lots of noise as we circled it. Then I heard that familiar crack of Harry's .22 rifle, and the second squirrel hit the ground.

I was now convinced that Nellie was the smartest dog in the world. But she had one more surprise for me that day.

After we killed several squirrels, Nellie disappeared for so long I thought she had gone home, but then she came back. This time she led us to a spot on a small ridge covered mostly with a variety of oak trees. Most of the leaves had fallen from the trees, but even still it was difficult to find a squirrel in some of the oaks.

Nellie positioned herself in front of the largest of the trees, a water oak. Harry and I took up our positions. I spotted what I thought was a squirrel, but wasn't sure. I told Harry I was going to waste a shell on it to find out. Sure enough, it was a squirrel.

Once again, Nellie did not leave. She kept pointing up that tree. It took a while of walking around the tree and shaking bushes, but the second squirrel finally moved, and Harry plugged it.

Instead of running off like she had in the past, Nellie just moved from the water oak to a different tree that was just a few yards away. She sat and patiently pointed to the top of the tree. Sure enough, we killed a third squirrel in the tree before the dog moved on.

We killed our bag limit of eight squirrels each that afternoon, and Nellie never lied once. She only took us to one tree, a cypress, in which we could not find a squirrel. The cypress had a hole in it where squirrels could hide. We could see the hole, but the dog couldn't. It was difficult to get the dog away from that tree, because Nellie knew there was a squirrel up it.

Nellie died before I went hunting with her again, but I never forgot what an amazingly smart dog she was. Although I no longer hunt animals, I have not seen or heard of a dog as smart as Nellie.

I never asked Harry's children about Nellie, but I expect they could tell some even more amazing stories about the time that Nellie was a part of their family.

Chapter 20 –
The Separation

All honorable men belong to the same tribe.

Indian Proverb

Of all the members of my family, Pee J.* (PJ for short) was the most subtle. He could stir up one member of the family, the whole family, or half the community. He was irresistible. No one argued with him; we accepted his ways as the gospel truth. PJ meant well, but in retrospect I can see that he put enmity in my heart and separated me from a part of society, preventing me from fully enjoying life. Well before I was born, PJ had established himself as a leader in my family; his influence upon my life was a source of inner conflict for many years; and when we finally separated it was an occasion for rejoicing.

When I arrived on the scene on November 9, 1938, PJ already had established himself quite firmly as one of the good ole boys in my parents' combined families of 17 living offspring, most of whom had already left the nest. I do not know when PJ was born, only that my parents had adopted him early in life. Although I could not see it as I grew up, PJ was not the smartest member of our family, even though he was much older, and perhaps that is why I and others in the family held him in such high esteem. PJ took to me early in life, as he had to my older brothers and sisters. When I went into the Air Force in January 1957, PJ's influence stuck to me like a birthmark.

The inner conflict caused by PJ's influence surfaced immediately after I arrived at Lackland Air Force Base in San Antonio, Texas. There were 72 men in my training flight, and scattered among the group were a number of people PJ had warned me not to associate with. I felt uneasy, especially when I learned that one of them, a hefty 200 pounder from Chicago who did not have an ounce of fat on his body, was to occupy the bunk immediately above the one I was to sleep in. I wanted to discuss the matter with the training instructor, but he was screaming and hollering at everybody, cussing and carrying on in such a way that I was afraid to say anything! I decided to live with the situation that night and bring it to the attention of the training instructor the first thing the next morning. But the next morning at 5 o'clock he came through the barracks hollering and screaming again. I never got the opportunity to say anything to him about these people sleeping in the same barracks with us, because he was always screaming and hollering and we were so busy there just wasn't time for anything else. Not only did I sleep in the same barracks with them, but I ate with them, took showers with them, and in general we lived together as if we were one big happy family. All of this was in direct violation of what PJ had taught me, and somehow I felt guilty and unclean for having violated his commands.

The inner conflict is what led to the eventual separation between me and PJ. The crack in his influence over me was made in 1958 at Dow Air Force Base in Bangor, Maine. I was enrolled in a speech course taught on base by a professor from the University of Maine at Orono. It was impromptu speech night and the professor, a Maniac who had no trouble recognizing my southern drawl, called upon me to defend some of the things that PJ had taught me to believe in. Realizing the importance of his assignment, the professor told me to take all the time I needed instead of the ten minutes he gave other students. It took me less than five minutes to defend what PJ had taught me on the subject he assigned. Before I left the podium, I knew deep down inside that I didn't fully understand everything PJ had said. After that night, I began to question everything that PJ had taught me. My questions only served to further widen the gap between us. My final confrontation with the teachings of PJ came in 1966 in Marysville, California. My family and I had become active in the Yuba City Church of Christ, and I was discovering that the Bible also disagrees with PJ's doctrine. The Bible teaches that a man cannot serve two masters. I decided then that I would no longer live according to PJ's gospel. This decision severed our ties, which had lasted for more than 27 years. I could rejoice at last, because I was finally free of his influence.

PJ comes back to haunt me occasionally, but I refuse to let his teachings influence my thinking. I know that his life is extended from generation to generation through those who simply accept him because that's the way it's always been and, if it was good enough for mamma and papa, it is good enough for me. But for those who dare question his doctrine, see the truth, and break away from him, there is joy in knowing they are no longer confined to sharing their life with one tribe, but with all of God's children no matter the color of their skin or where they come from.

*A pseudonym for prejudice

Chapter 21 –
Tears of Joy

My emotions on the morning of January 5, 1957, were on a roller coaster. My brother Harry was to pick me up at 9:30 and take me to the train station in Rocky Mount, North Carolina. I was leaving home to find out what life offered beyond my parents' farm in the Islands of Martin County, North Carolina.

I was learning that talking about leaving home and actually leaving was quite different. Surfacing that morning were memories that were absent during the talking stage, and they were making it much more difficult than I had imagined to say good-bye to my family. This was especially true of my mother. With my father, that was another story.

Love was not a word that I remember my father ever using. In his lifetime I cannot recall him ever saying to me or any of my brothers and sisters: "I love you." Nor did he ever go out of his way to show any affection for me. For example, he never gave me a birthday present or a gift for Christmas. He never sang happy birthday to me or spoke any words of praise to me directly.

Dad was a quiet man. I remember working with him all day, in a drizzling rain, and not hearing him say more than a few dozen words. "Bring the hammer and nails." "Get me the water." "Time for dinner." "That's it." "Let's go." That was about the day's conversation unless someone asked him a question.

He expected a great deal from me and always assumed that I knew what to do. If I was on the other end of a crosscut saw, he expected me to pull when it came my way and to push when it was going in the other direction. If we were putting up a wire fence, I had better be doing something to help get that fence stretched and nailed to the posts. He expected me to work all the time and he made sure that I never ran out of jobs.

By the time I turned 16, I began to suspect that dad looked at me as a farm hand rather than as a son. Unless it was raining, most mornings I was up in time to do an hour's work before going to school. As soon as I returned from school I had to change clothes and work until dark, and then feed the hogs, cows, and mules before eating supper. During the summer, we worked from sun-up to sun-down, and it was rare that we ate supper before 8 or 8:30 p.m. My father believed that weekends were made for working. Somehow he always managed to squeeze more daylight out of Saturday than any other day of the week. He was not a religious man, but he did believe in resting on the first day of the week.

However, for me Sunday was not a total day of rest. I still had to feed the farm animals on Sunday, and if they escaped from their pen or pasture my brothers and I had to chase them until we got them back in and mend the broken fences. It seems that at least once a month, and usually on Sunday, we spent half the day chasing animals and fixing fences.

The year after I turned 16, dad decided to tend 100 acres of land. Actually, it was my older brother Dallas and I and one antiquated Farmall C tractor that would be doing the farming; dad would just make sure that we did it his way, which, like the old tractor, was behind the times. The next year Dallas married and moved on and the 100 acres was left to me and that Farmall C.

I attempted to attend Jamesville High School and farm too. It didn't work. My grades suffered and it got to the point where I felt like a stranger at school. Dad could not read or write and did not encourage me to go to school. It seemed to me that he was more interested in me taking care of the farm than he was in my education. In November 1956 I dropped out of the 11th grade, and the following month, after harvesting all the crops, I talked to the local Air Force recruiter. My decision to quit school and join the Air Force did not set well with mom, but dad said nothing; I really didn't think he cared what I did.

The thought of leaving home without knowing how dad felt about me weighed heavily on my mind as I packed a few belongings in a small bag for the train ride to Lackland Air Force Base in Texas. There was a lump in my throat that was not eased any by mom's presence and the tears in her eyes. I tried to reassure her that everything would be okay, but it was no use.

When Harry came to pick me up, I had said good-bye to mamma in the house. Then I went out into the front yard where dad was standing. He had not said anything all morning.

It took me a few minutes to stop the tears that had come so easily from saying good-bye to mom. But as I approached my dad I really didn't know what to say. As I walked toward him, he reached into the left front pocket of his pants and pulled out his tattered, black purse. He opened it and retrieved a $20 bill, handed it to me, and asked if that would be enough. It was the first time he had given me money without me having to ask for it.

I had not expected anything, so I was grateful for the extra money. I answered that it would be enough and thanked him for it.

I realized then that, even though we had never been very close, that deep down inside I loved him. He wished me good luck as he shook my hand, and even though I was beginning to get that lump in my throat again, I still did not see any emotional change in dad. As I went to get into Harry's pickup, I took one final look over my shoulder and saw my father reach for his pocket handkerchief to wipe away the tears that were trickling down his wrinkled cheeks. Without saying a word, my father had answered an important question for me that morning.

As we pulled away from the good earth and place where I had been nurtured for the first 18 years of my life, I could not hold back the tears which brought me relief and joy from knowing that my father loved me.

Years later I realized that while leaving home was a first for me, dad had witnessed it many times. He had seen 18 other children or stepchildren go before me. The last member of the clan would leave two years later.

Dad died on March 4, 1968, of a heart attack. The night before his death, he had severe chest pains, but would not let his grandson Herbert go and get my brother Dallas to take him to the doctor until the next morning. On the way to the doctor's office, dad insisted on stopping first at Martin Supply to pay a bill. Dallas tried to persuade him to remain in the truck while he paid the bill, but dad insisted on going in to pay it himself. When he got out of the truck, Dallas was there to lend a hand. Dad collapsed and died in Dallas' arms.

Mom with granddaughters Kay, right, and Jinny in wheelbarrow with grandson Dean. Mom never met a kid she didn't love.

Chapter 22 –
Memories of Mom's Death

On January 1, 1991, my sister Mary M. Myers and her husband Bob were visiting with our brother Dallas and his wife Peggy, who still live on the family farm, and other relatives in the area. My wife Mary, and I, who live in Goldsboro, drove to the farm that day to visit with them and other family members.

Sis, as she was called when we grew up together, left home when she was a junior in high school, and we have not seen each other much since then.

During our visit we talked politics, about events in the Persian Gulf, and our days on the farm. However, what I remember most about that day was our conversation about mom and her death.

Mom was superstitious. She carried a rabbit's foot with her at all times for good luck. And she also carried in another pocket a buckeye as an extra measure of good luck. In fact, I have the buckeye that she was carrying when she died. And I plan to pass it on to our granddaughter, not that I believe it will bring her good luck, but so she will have something to connect her with the past, with a person she never met, but someone from whom she received some of her genes.

Although I don't remember playing with frogs, we had plenty of them around and I would occasionally come in contact with one. Whether that is where my warts came from I do not know, but mom's formula for getting rid of them may seem strange today, but it didn't back then.

On the first night of a full moon, she told me to keep my head down, walk out into the yard, then look up at the moon, and while looking at the moon pick up something on the ground, rub it on the wart or warts and throw it over my shoulder. If the wart was on my left hand or arm I would throw whatever I rubbed on it over my left shoulder, and vice versa. After I had accomplished this, I was to return to the house without looking at the moon again and forget about the warts. In just a few days my warts were gone. Did it work, or did my warts just happen to decide to leave on their own? I don't know, and I have not had any warts since to try the formula again. Until I do, I must believe that it was a success, because some of my siblings used it with the same results.

There was another remedy, too, that was used then, but is not found in medical text books today. When my brother, Lester, was accidentally hit just above his right eye with an axe, leaving a huge gash, I was instructed to go upstairs and collect all the cobwebs I could find. This I did, and mom put the cobwebs on the cut where it stayed until he was transported to the doctor's office in Williamston.

Sis was very close to mom and recalled the last time she visited her. Sis said that mom had told her she might not be around much longer. "But I didn't take it seriously," Sis said.

As our discussion continued, we began to recall other things that had happened to us before mom's death.

Sis said she had a dream in which she was standing in the front yard of the house in which we were raised. She recalled that as she stood there, the walnut tree in the front yard fell on mom and killed her. She said she screamed and ran to the tree and tried to lift it off mom but could not.

The day after that dream, she received a phone call informing her that our older half brother, Dennis, had died of cancer. Dennis died February 12, 1967. Sis said mom was doing fine then.

About a month later, Sis said she had a premonition that something was wrong. It just came over her like a dark cloud. Sis said she was going to call mom that very night, but the phone was busy and she became involved with other family matters and didn't get around to it.

The next day, March 24, 1967, Sis learned what it was that her dreams were trying to tell her. She would not get a chance to talk with mom again. The call she received that day was to inform her that mom had died in her sleep with a smile on her face. Our brother's son, Marty, had slept with her that night. She was 64 years old. Her death was a shock to everyone.

I was on the Island of Guam in the Western Pacific, but I also had a dream, a forewarning that something terrible was going to happen. The only difference between my dream and the one Sis had is that I could not remember what mine was about.

What I do remember is that it was the most horrible dream I had ever had in my life, and I refused to even try to remember it afterwards. When I awoke the morning after the dream, I erased it from my memory, and for once it worked, because I have never remembered any of the details of that dream.

What I do remember about the dream is that a week or so afterwards, I received a call to report to the Red Cross Office on base. I immediately went. Since Dennis had died a month earlier,

I suspected that dad may have passed on since he was getting on in years.

The lady at the Red Cross Office invited me to sit down in the chair beside her desk. She very gently told me she had some bad news for me. And when she told me that mom had died, I nearly fell out of the chair. The first thing I thought of when she told me mom had died was the dream—the dream was my warning that something terrible was about to happen, but even the dream could not prepare me for this news.

Sis told of the grief that mom's death had brought to her and how she tried not to grieve because she had been told that grieving keeps the dead person from going on to better things and a better life. She said she did not want to keep mamma here any longer, but she could not help but grieve over her death.

"Sometimes I felt that if I could turn around fast enough I would see mamma standing behind me," Sis recalled. She told of dreaming about her and asking if she were okay, and "Mama would smile and wave to me. I once dreamed that she kissed me and when I awoke my cheek was moist as if someone had kissed me."

The wonderful memories we shared that day of mom brought tears of joy to both of us. We were not grieving over our loss, but remembering what a blessing we had in our mother. We did not want her to return to this life because we both believed this was her hell. And we believed she was in a place of peace and that she was content and happy. We did not want our tears to disturb that condition, not for our mother.

It was a good day, that January 1st, 1991. The crisis in the Persian Gulf did not stop us from remembering our unsung heroine at this season of Ole Lang Syne. Mom was our warrior, our defender from all enemies, foreign and domestic, the one who did her very best to keep us on the straight and narrow road. Her love for us was not expressed in words, but in every deed she ever did for us. She won our hearts and our admiration; she was our inspiration; we could not ask God for a better mother.

Chapter 23 –
Unforgettable Moments

Everyone has those moments in life that are unforgettable. Many of those moments are the same for everyone, i.e., marriage, the birth of children, grandchildren, and graduations. But there are some unforgettable moments that are as unique to each of us as our fingerprints, DNA or the sounds of our voices.

Few take the time to look back, find those special times, and ponder their impact on their lives.

My first unforgettable moment in life came at a revival meeting at Reddicks Grove Baptist Church in Williams Township of Martin County, North Carolina, in 1949. It was the closest church to where my parents lived, and while my parents were not particularly religious folk, they did attend church services occasionally and tried to attend the annual week-long revival that ended with dinner on the grounds. It was the one week in the year when every seat in the church was filled every night. Just about every member showed up at revival time, either for spiritual renewal or fellowship or both. The parking area around the church would be filled with mules and wagons and carts and a few automobiles and trucks. There was great preaching and singing and an outstanding feast on Sunday. Folks in the community got to know each other a little better that week and there were always a few who came forward to accept Christ and were baptized following the dinner on the grounds.

I saw myself as a very poor country boy and was so shy that I thought even my shadow was watching me! My mother always encouraged me to read the Bible but beyond that there were no Bible instructions, no prayers, and no explanation of the plan of salvation in my home. I heard about the Lord mostly in ungodly terms and saw the devil at work on a regular basis. God's name was seldom praised, but often used in vain. If curse words could have turned into flowers, our home and yard would have been a beautiful place. In fact, I don't know if we would have had any land left to plant crops!

During the revival of 1949, I made the most important decision of my life. This shy ten-year-old kid got up from his pew during the invitation, walked down the isle with a church full of people watching, stood before the congregation and accepted Christ as his Savior. I did not make this decision based on what my friends were doing, because I cannot name one of the others who came forward that week. My parents had not encouraged me to go forward. I did not accept Christ out of fear of going to hell. I don't know why I got up and went down that isle; I just got up and did it. I don't even remember being scared. After my baptism, I had this feeling inside that I had done something good, something very special.

As I round the last bend in the road of my life and look back, I realize just how important that decision was. No, I have not always done what God wanted me to do, but God knew that when He called me out of that pew. It has taken God a long time, and while watching over me and my family all these years and providing me and my family with everything we need and much more, He has molded me into a human being that is far better than the one He started with. He has cleansed my heart of the poisons of this world such as malice, prejudice, and hatred, and He has filled it with the fruit of the Spirit—love, joy, peace, patience, kindness, goodness, and faithfulness.

Another unforgettable moment in my life occurred in 1955. I was in the tenth grade and, on this particular day, a cousin offered me a ride to school. On the way to Jamesville we decided to spend the day riding around. This was the first time I had skipped school, and I was confident that no one would ever find out. I was dead wrong.

When I came home that afternoon, I went into the kitchen. Mom was standing over the wood stove cooking. She turned her head and looked at me with tears in her eyes and asked, "Why didn't you go to school today?" That's all that was ever said about that missed day of school, but it was enough. My mother's tears were more powerful than any words she could speak or a severe beating. I realized at that moment that I had hurt the one person in the world who loved me more than anyone else and it nearly broke my heart. I promised myself then and there that I would never again do something to hurt mom. And I didn't.

Events that brought much grief to mom rolled into her life like summer storms. There was the time when dad gave her a black eye and hunted her for three days because he believed she had stolen some of his money. This near-death event nearly drained all the spirit from her life, but she eventually bounced back, and a much later event that impacted her, too, would vindicate her as the innocent victim of dad's wrath.

Mom raised my nephew Melvin McCandless until he was old enough to start school; he was like a brother to me and like a son to mom. When the day came for Melvin to go home with his mom and stepfather, he did not want to go. And we didn't want him to go. But we had no choice.

That Sunday afternoon, with the car packed with his belongings, Melvin refused to get into the car. Someone asked me to get in the car and ride with Melvin down the road a ways and then get out. Reluctantly, I agreed and Melvin reluctantly crawled in beside me. A short distance down the road, they stopped the car and I got out and returned home with tears in my eyes. Melvin stayed in the car.

Even though there was nothing we could have done to stop him from leaving, I have always felt that I betrayed Melvin that day. Mom and I cried for days afterward. Melvin would return to live with mom and dad and finish high school in Jamesville. Although I was not there at the time, I know that it made mom happy.

One of the saddest moments in mom's life, and maybe the saddest, was the morning she awoke and found that her youngest daughter, Mary, had quit the eleventh grade and left home to marry a man in Texas. She had been communicating with him by mail and secretly planning her departure. She left a note telling mom what she had done. Shock, unbelief, sadness, and a sense of hopelessness filled mom's heart for days afterward. And I did not think she would ever stop crying. The sadness we all experienced is only secondary to the grief that we saw mom endure. Two beautiful granddaughters, Gwen and Kay, came from this marriage and brought mom joy as she kept them for a number of years, but then they returned to their mom and stepfather, once again bringing mom more grief.

One other unforgettable moment came in 1965, shortly after I arrived at Beale Air Force Base in California. One Sunday afternoon I was writing a letter to mom on my Royal typewriter, when suddenly out of the clear blue sky I came to the realization that I had never told my mother that I loved her. "I love you" was a sentence that I never heard when I grew up. We were just supposed to know that we loved certain people; we didn't have to say it. When I closed my letter that day, I ended it with: "I love you, mom." And then I cried.

What I now realize is that as we travel through life, events beyond our control will bring us heartache. They will stand out among all the joyous occasions. But they will not defeat us unless we let them. I saw my mom go down many times, but she got up before the count of ten and rallied to fight another day. She carried her burdens like a true champion, she did not abandon her family because the road was hard, and she did not weigh herself down with malice, anger, hate, and revenge.

I love you, mom.

Chapter 24 –
Memories of Dad

Although dad and I were not real close, I have many fond memories of him. He would take me coon hunting, and while I don't remember us ever killing a coon, I do remember riding on his back, holding the lantern in one hand and his 12-gauge shotgun in the other, as he held me and waded across swamps in water three feet deep. Dad was a drinker and I could smell the alcohol on his breath. While I was afraid at times that we were lost in the swamps, we always returned safely to our home. We also fished together, and while I did not realize it at the time, I waded through the swamps with him to mark the boundaries of the land that he willed to me before his death. I also remember the times he would take me to town with him along with a wagon load of watermelons he would sell.

Dad was not much of a talker, but he had some sayings which I have not forgotten. Speaking of those who did not work, he would remark, "They want a job with the work picked out of it." Or, "You can't help a man who won't help himself." Or, "They want something for nothing."

While he was not rich, he was the source of money for many of the folk in the area who could not borrow the time of day from a bank. They would come to him—older children, grandchildren, neighbors, both black and white—wanting to borrow a dollar or two. If he had it, and he usually did, dad would loan them the money, knowing that he would probably never see it again.

Dad was not one who attended church on a regular basis. However, when preachers visited him he would give them money for the offering, or he would send money with someone else to put in the offering plate. When our black neighbors came and asked for a piece of pork to cook with their collards, he would always oblige.

When I was born, dad was less than two months away from celebrating his 61st birthday. I watched him plow corn and peanuts in the heat of summer with mules when he was 70. Dad was a blacksmith, and a good one, too. When he purchased his first Farmall C tractor, he built the plows used for cultivating corn and peanuts. I operated the bellows that kept the coals hot for heating the iron and watched him bend the iron bars into shape and make the holes for the bolts. If anything broke down that could be fixed, dad could usually fix it, and haywire was the duct tape of that era. If a tool needed a handle, he made it, and the one he made was not as easy to break as the ones purchased from Martin Supply.

Dad wore long johns year round. He said they kept him cool in summer and warm in winter. He would work until noon, eat dinner, take a two-hour nap, get up and work until dark. His favorite day of the week to work was Saturday; that was the day the kids were out of school. I believe that when he was napping he was dreaming up jobs for us kids on Saturday. Sunday was a day of rest unless the animals escaped from their pens. It's amazing how fast a horse or mule can return to its wild roots once it escapes from its stall.

He never learned to drive any of the tractors; he left that chore to the younger generation.

I believe dad was one of the more prosperous farmers in the county, although he never boasted about what he owned. In fact, I don't believe he realized how much wealth he had accumulated.

Dad could not read and in some places his signature on documents was an "X" while on others he managed to write "W.F. Barber." But he was a smart man in many ways. He took advantage of the opportunities that came his way. He was tough. He worked hard. A gang of children helped him to accumulate his property. He knew the value of a dollar; the kids did not get an allowance; they had to beg for what they got. I do not ever remember his trying to swindle anyone out of anything, or trying to pull anything over on someone for personal gain. Except for making and selling illicit alcohol during the depression, he earned every dollar he made honestly.

It took me a long time to realize that dad was quite a remarkable man. No one ever told me I was blind when I was a kid, but if they had, I would not have believed them. It was not until I left home and looked back at what I had been privileged to be a part of that I realized how lucky I was. When I left home, I expected nothing more than what my parents had already given me. And yet, dad thought enough of me to give me more than 150 acres of land. I cherish this gift, not because it is all that valuable as farm land, but because it represents the sacrifices my parents made, not for themselves, but for me.

I left home not knowing how much I loved my dad That love has grown over the years as I have come to better understand him and his generation, which grew up under far more difficult circumstances than mine. And although I never expressed it to him, I am extremely grateful for every thing he and mom did for me. And I pray that both forgave me for my ungratefulness during that time when I could not see.

Chapter 25 –
Your Reward for Reading This Book

If you have found your way to this chapter, you deserve a reward—even if you didn't read all of the previous 24 chapters! The recipe below is my favorite from among the many delicious meals mom cooked for our family. I didn't know how good mom's cooking was until I left home. In all my travels, from England to Japan and many points in between, I never saw this recipe on any menus, and I never met anyone outside of North Carolina who had even heard of it.

Mom never put any of her recipes in writing—they all came from memory. These measurements are approximate, so you are free to make adjustments to suit your palate. This gourmet meal consists of chocolate, biscuits, and fried country ham or sausage or both, and we washed it down with real cow's milk, coffee, water or iced tea. You don't have to make the biscuits from scratch like mom did, and besides, the ones you buy will be just as good with a little extra chocolate on them!

In summer, when mom had the windows open in the kitchen, I could smell the ham cooking all the way down to the barn some 75 yards away. So, you may want to keep your windows closed, or plan to feed the neighbors when you cook this meal!

The recipe for chocolate:

3 cups of sugar

5 heaping tablespoons of cocoa

Mix the chocolate and sugar in an iron frying pan until smooth

Stir in one 12-ounce can of evaporated milk (low-fat is okay)

Add about 6 ounces of water and one-eighth teaspoon of salt

Bring to a boil on medium high heat

After it boils, turn heat down to medium low

Cook until foam disappears

Stir frequently from the time pan begins to heat up until it is cooked

After it is cooked and you have turned the heat off, add 2 teaspoons of Vanilla

Add 2 tablespoons of butter

The chocolate will be syrupy when cooked. Pour it over a buttered hot biscuit and enjoy, along with your country ham or sausage, and beverage of choice.

One other thing about this meal, you won't need a dessert afterwards!

This recipe feeds six to eight hungry adults if you have plenty of ham and sausage and biscuits to go with it.

The author is not responsible for any weight you might gain from pigging out on this meal!

PART II

PATERNAL FAMILY HISTORY

Great Grandparents

The 1850 census of Martin County, North Carolina, lists Henry Barber, born in 1820, and Emily Barber, born in 1821, as having four children:

Sarah Jane Barber – born in 1847

Benjamin Barber – born in 1848

Martha Barber – born in 1850

Annie Barber – born in 1852 (She was listed as a servant in the home of Zack Gurkin in the 1880 census,)

The 1860 census listed the value of Henry Barber's real estate at $100.00. It also listed his wife's name as Mary. Her full name was Mary Emily Barber. I have no information on her maiden name or their months and dates of birth or when they died. It is not known where they are buried, and the Barber burial plot does not have any grave markers with their names on them. The Barber burial plot is located off Highway 171 south of Jamesville. Directions: turn left off Highway 171 onto Manning Road. The graveyard is located on the right in a curve between Barber Road and Barber Cutoff Road.

He was a farmer in Jamesville Township.

No Barbers were listed on the 1840 census in Martin County, so Henry and Emily apparently were the first Barbers to settle in the county. I do not know where they came from but suspect that they moved to Martin County from another county in North Carolina.

The area in Jamesville Township where they lived later became known as the Barber Neighborhood, probably because so many of them were born in the area and stayed there.

Records show that Henry served in the Civil War and died in Lynchburg, Virginia. According to James H. McCallum, MD, a Pvt. Henry Barber from Martin County served in the Civil War from June 17, 1861, to February 1863, when he died in Lynchburg, Virginia. This information is recorded on page 129 of his book, *Martin County during the Civil War*, on file in the library in Williamston. The census records for Martin County during this period listed only one Henry Barber who was 40 years of age in 1861. No one in the family ever mentioned that we had a relative who served in the Civil War. I do not know if Henry died in battle or as a prisoner of war. He served with Company H, 1st Regiment, North Carolina Troops, Infantry, and the unit was called "Bagley Guards."

Henry is not listed in the 1870 census, only his wife and children. For some reason, all the ages are incorrect: Emily was 49, not 40; Sarah Jane was 23, not 18; Benjamin was 22, not 14; Martha was 20, not 12; and Annie was 18, not 10. Annie was also called Amy in the 1870 census. Emily's real estate was valued at $50.00.

Grandparents

Benjamin T. Barber was born December 26, 1848, and Mary Emily (also listed in places as Emmerline, Emeline and Emma) Gardner Barber was born March 16, 1855. They were married on March 19, 1874. The marriage register for the years 1872-1896, Page 6, in the Register of Deeds Office in Williamston notes that when they were married Benjamin (no middle name or initial listed) was 21 years old and Emmerline was 17 years and four months. If they were born on the dates indicated, they were 26 and 19, respectively. They were married by J.J. Smith at T. Gardner's (probably her parents' home). Emily died March 8, 1923; Benjamin's date of death is unknown but the 1910 census indicates that he died around 1904 or 1905. It is unknown where they are buried, and the Barber burial plot has no grave markers with their names on them. They lived on the corner of Manning Road and Barber Cutoff Road, a short distance from the Barber burial plot where it is believed they are buried. This graveyard has many grave markers without names. The Barber Cemetery, or burial plot, is owned by Shirley Barber Lilley. The graveyard is listed as the Roberson Cemetery in some places. It was probably owned previously by the Roberson family, some of whom are buried there.

Children from this marriage:

Sarah C. Barber – July 28, 1875 – September 24, 1875

Lula V. Barber – October 7, 1876 – date of death unknown

William Frank Barber – December 27, 1877 – March 4, 1968

Emma Della Barber – November 15, 1879 – date of death unknown

Hoyt B. Barber – August 5, 1881 – November 25, 1933

Henry W. Barber – September 27, 1883 – March 9, 1945

Alonzo M. Barber – August 28, 1887 – January 28, 1924

Warren S. Barber – June 9, 1888 – November 2, 1934

Sylvester Clyde Barber – February 9, 1890 – died in Richmond, Virginia

Perlie C. Barber – December 13, 1892 – April 30, 1966

Martha G. Barber – May 13, 1894 – date of death unknown

Rusian M. Barber – March 13, 1896 – date of death unknown

Father

William Frank Barber was born in Jamesville Township to Benjamin T. and Mary Emily (also listed in some places as Emmerline, Emeline and Emma) Gardner Barber on December 27, 1877, and died March 4, 1968. The 1880 census listed him as Franklin Barber and this could be his middle name. The gravestone where Lizzie, his second wife, is buried is also marked for W.F. Barber, assuming that he would be buried with her. That stone lists his year of birth as 1876, as does his obituary. However, this is incorrect. His sister Lula was born in October 1876 so he could not have been born two months later. He lived to be 91. He was buried in Martin Memorial Gardens off Highway 64 between Williamston and Everetts with his third wife, Icelene.

First Marriage

Although not recorded in the marriage registers in the Register of Deeds Office in the courthouse in Williamston, the 1900 census notes that Frank had been married to a woman named Jesse, last name unknown, for five years. He married her around 1895, and it is believed that she died while giving birth to their first child, which also died. Her death occurred after the 1900 census was taken. Frank and Jesse lived next door to his parents' home in Jamesville Township and according to the census Frank was a manual laborer. There is no record of Jesse's death or her burial, but she was probably buried in the Barber Cemetery which is located less than half a mile from where they lived. The graveyard has numerous unmarked grave sites. Since Frank lived in Norfolk in his early years, it is possible that Jesse was from the Norfolk area and it is also possible that he carried her back to that area for burial.

Second Marriage and Children

William F. Barber married Lizzie Rowena Simpson on September 11, 1901. She was born September 12, 1882, and died May 22, 1931, at the age of 49 of cancer of the stomach. She had suffered with the disease for about two years, and several months before her death had an operation that provided some relief. She died at home. On her gravestone, in the Barber burial plot, her last name is spelled Simason. This is incorrect. They were married in the home of Lizzie's parents, Major and Margaret Simpson. Their marriage certificate notes that he was 22 and Lizzie was 18. Since he was born in 1877, he was 23 in September 1901. Based on her date of birth, Lizzie's age is correct; she was one day shy of her 19th birthday. The marriage ceremony was conducted by Jas. (James?) W. Hardison, MLS. The Simpson family lived in Jamesville Township. Other Simpson family children were Mary, Ludie, Charles, Agnus (Gertie) and Beulah. Dad's brothers Hoyt and Perlie married Ludie and Beulah, respectively.

Children from this marriage:

June 11, 1902 – April 30, 1977, Lula Barber, 74; Lula married C. W. Bembridge, age 49, on January 11, 1920. The marriage certificate indicates that Lula was 18. If her age is correct on the marriage certificate, she would have been born in 1902, nine months after her parents were married, and not 1900 as reported in her obituary. She had five children by her first husband, Charlie: Charlie (Bud), Hazel, Ervin, Eugene, and Fanny (Allie). She and her second husband, Arthur Lilley, had four children: Russell, Bruce, Loraine and Arthur, Jr.

October 25, 1903 – February 12, 1967, Dennis Roosevelt Barber, 63; he died of lung cancer. He married Essie Mae Perry February 21, 1926. His age on the marriage register was given as 21 and Essie's as 18. I suspect he was 22, not 21, and his date of birth given in his obituary was incorrect. The 1910 census lists Dennis' age as 7, which means he would have been born in 1903 and not 1902. Dennis and Essie had seven children: Louis, Hubert, Grover, Carroll, Garland, Paul, and Ruth.

October 12, 1904 – January 25, 1994, Tillie Barber, 89. Her obituary states she was born in Norfolk, Virginia. She was married to Walter Barnes. They had seven children: Gladys, Doris, Walter, Jr., Hazel, William, Raymond, and James.

September 16, 1907 – May 15, 1980 - Chrish Malcolm Barber, 72. He was married on December 27, 1927, his dad's 49th birthday. He was called Toby. He is buried in Oakdale Cemetery with his wife Della in Washington, N.C. His daughter Leta said he spelled his first name Chrish and his middle name was Malcolm. In numerous places it is spelled Chris. Toby and Della had six children: James, Leta Marie, Douglas, Kenneth, Thurman, and Marvin.

1908 – April 3, 1934 – Maggie Mae (also May in some places) Barber was murdered by her husband Joe Davenport at the age of 26. She was buried in the Barber Cemetery beside her mother in Jamesville. She was listed as being four years old in the 1910 census. Assuming her age is correct in this census report, she would have been born in 1906 and not 1908. In the newspaper account of her murder, her age is listed as 26, which I believe is correct. The 1920 census listed her age as 10, and that is incorrect because she certainly was not born in 1910. She married Joseph F. Davenport January 31, 1926; his age was listed as 51 and hers as 17. Both ages are incorrect. If she were born in 1908 then she would have been 15 or 16. Her first child, Herbert, was born out of wedlock on November 14, 1924, at which time she was 14 or 15. No birth certificate or other record of birth could be found on Maggie. She and Joe had four children: Edward, Gilbert, Clifton, and Elizabeth.

May 12, 1911 – April 1, 2000, Effie Barber, 88. She married Harvey C. Perry on May 5, 1928, at the age of 17. No middle name was listed in the record of this marriage. Harvey, born May 30, 1909, was a laborer at the North Carolina Pulp Company in Plymouth and was killed in an accident August 20, 1941. An electrical shock caused him to fall from a loft to the concrete floor some 20 feet below in one of the buildings at the mill. His head was crushed from the fall, and it was never determined if he died from the electrical shock or the fall. He was buried the next day in the Reddicks Grove Baptist Church Cemetery. He was 32 years old. The 1920 census listed a Maye E. Barber as being 7 years old. This person has to be Effie. The only question is if her first name was Maye as listed on the census; no one ever called her Maye, it was always Effie. Children from the marriage to Perry were Eva Gray (better known as Janie), Mildred, Elmer, Ralph, Alfred, Henry and Noah. Effie married George Alfred Hardison, 39, December 19, 1942. They had two children: Gene and Peggy.

March 12, 1915 – July 18, 1994. William Harry Barber, 79. In some places his year of birth is listed as 1914. The 1920 census lists a William Barber as being four years old at the time. I believe this is William Harry Barber, although there's a couple of years difference in ages of Harry Barber and the William listed in the census. He married Kathleen Bailey on December 4, 1939, in Chesterfield County, Virginia. Harry and Kathleen were step brother and sister. They had five children: Betty Jean, Harry, Jr., Sammy, Millie, and Ricky.

1915-1919 – Lizzie Margaret Barber. This information was taken from the gravestone where she is buried beside her mother. If Harry was born March 12, she would have had to be born in November or December of 1915. No record of her birth or her death could be found.

October 25, 1919 – May 18, 1977, Benjamin Franklin Barber, 57. On his birth certificate he is listed as William Franklin Barber. His date of death is listed as October 19 on his grave stone. This is incorrect. He and Major were twins. Ben died of cancer. He and his wife Elizabeth had three children: Marie, Alice, and Benjamin.

October 25, 1919 – May 4, 1989, William Major Barber, 69; Major and Ben were twins. Major was married to Frances Williams. They had three sons: Major Earl, Tony, and Jody. Frances was killed in an auto accident Friday, June 23, 2006, near Gardner Creek. She was buried in the Barber Cemetery located on the farm that she and Major owned off Highway 64. She was 73 years old.

January 3, 1921 – December 25, 1992, Clyde Barber; 71. Clyde married Mildred Irene Moore on December 6, 1941. Mildred was born September 27, 1924. They had three children: Lizzie Irene, Faye, and Clyde Melvin.

April 21, 1923 – June 27, 1973, Emily (Emeline) Barber, 50; on her birth certificate she is listed as a twin. On the birth certificate both children were listed as Emeline Barber, and both were listed as being alive when they were born. Apparently the other twin died shortly after birth. She was called Emmy or Emily. Emily died in Portsmouth, Virginia. She was married to Leroy Knox. They had four sons: Roy Franklin, Odell, Billy Joe, and James.

August 2, 1923 – There is one birth certificate on file in the Register of Deeds Office in Williamston, N.C., that lists a child born to Frank and Lizzie Barber on this date. It was listed as a twin. The child was stillborn. As a child I heard that my father and Lizzie had three sets of twins, and that one set died at birth. This must have been the set that died, and no wonder; these births came less than four months after delivering her second set of twins, one of whom died. A grave marker for this set of twins is placed beside their mother and sisters in the Barber Cemetery in Jamesville.

February 24, 1926 – October 21, 1974, Henry Hoyt Barber, 48. He was killed by a stepdaughter of a shotgun blast to the stomach during a family argument. On his birth certificate, Hoyt is spelled Hoyte, which is incorrect. He and his wife Marie had one son: Henry, Jr.

Illegitimate Children
December 28, 1909 - December 5, 2004, James Arthur Barber, son of William F. Barber and Gertie A. Simpson, sister of his wife Lizzie. Arthur and Robert were full brothers. He died December 5, 2004, in Guardian Care Nursing Home in Scotland Neck, North Carolina. He was 23 days shy of his 95th birthday. Gertie

was just 17 years old when Arthur was born. Arthur and his wife Rena had five sons: Donald, Gene Autry (Bobby), Frank, Tim, and Kenneth.

July 16, 1912 – September 20, 1994, Robert Clifton Barber, 82. He was the son of William F. Barber and Gertie A. Simpson, sister of his wife Lizzie. He and Arthur were full brothers. He died in Richmond, Virginia. Gertie was two months shy of her 20th birthday when Robert was born. Robert and his wife Eleanor had five children: Bobby, Melvin, Gloria, Phyllis, and Cecelia.

Arthur and Robert were raised by Frank and Lizzie, and they were the only two children in the family to stay with Frank until they were 21-years-old. In the 1930 census they are listed as boarders in the Frank and Lizzie Barber home and their last names are listed as Simpson. It is not known when they changed their last name to Barber.

The final four children born to Frank and Icelene Barber, from left, are Dallas, Lester, Jasper, and Mary, c. 1980.

Third Marriage and Children

William F. Barber married Icelene Davenport Bailey (also spelled Isolene, Isoline, and Icelean) on November 22, 1931. He was 35 days shy of his 55th birthday and Icelene was 29. They were married in Williamston by Justice of the Peace J.L. Hassue. Witnesses were C.C. Daniel and J.E. Manning.

Children from this marriage:

April 19, 1933, Dallas H. Barber. He married Peggy Price. They had four children: Mitchell, Billy, Jeanette and Robbie.

May 25, 1935, Mary M. Barber; her birth certificate on file in the Register of Deeds Office in Williamston, North Carolina, does not include her name. She married Richard Don Rogers of Texas in 1952. They had two daughters, Donna Kay and Jinny (Gwen). She divorced Rogers and married Bob Myers.

November 9, 1938, Jasper E. Barber. He married Mary J. Rogers of Brewer, Maine, October 2, 1959. They had two sons: Dean and Larry.

May 16, 1940 – May 16, 2003, Lester H. Barber; he committed suicide. He was married three times and had three children by his second wife Janie: Marty, Patty, and Regina. Patty committed suicide in Paris, Texas, October 20, 1994, at the age of 31.

Total Number of Children

From marriage to Maggie: 16 – One daughter, Lizzie, died at age three or four; one twin died at birth and one set of twins were born dead; 12 of the 16 children survived, married and had children.

Children born out of wedlock to William F. Barber and Maggie's sister, Gertie A. Simpson: two. Both married and had children.

From marriage to Icelene: 4. All married and had children.

From Icelene's marriage to her first husband Raleigh Bailey: two. Both married and had children.

Grand total: 24 (including the four deceased children)

MATERNAL FAMILY HISTORY

Great Grandparents

My great grandparents were John and Mary A. Webb (Web in some places). They are first listed in the 1870 census. John was listed as being 29 years of age and Mary as 23. They had one son, John Jr., age 1.

The 1880 census lists John and Mary A. Webb as having five children:

John D., age 10; Joseph C., age 8; Larrance, age 5; Mozella (spelled Mozlar and Mosella in some places) age 3; and Ida E., age 1. This census also notes that John Webb was 30 years old and Mary was 25. The family lived in Bear Grass, North Carolina, in the home of Daniel Rogerson. I believe the ages are incorrect in the 1880 census. If the ages are correct in the 1870 census, John would be 39 and Mary 33 in 1880.

The 1880 census also lists a Joseph Webb, age 60, a widowed farmer living with his daughter Martha, age 40. If kin to John, it is unknown how they were related.

The 1900 census listed Mary A. Webb, age 47, born in November 1853, as being the head of the household, and two children living in the household: Sylvester, born in May 1882, and a daughter Eaver, age 13, born in December 1888. I suspect this was my great grandmother and that her husband had died. However, her age is not consistent with the 1870 census which indicates she was born in 1847, making her 53 years old in 1900 and not 47.

Mozella Webb Gardner, c. 1930; the only photo the author could locate of a grandparent, copied from the original owned by Glenn Koepp, his second cousin.

Grandparents

Mozella Webb was born July 11, 1877, and died of a stroke on Sunday morning, November 8, 1936, at the age of 59. She had had two light strokes previous to the one that took her life. My Aunt Mary Fleming said her mother had sent her to the garden to get a herb she grew that was used to relieve pain. Mary said that when she returned, her mother fell over on her and died. She died at her home in Bear Grass.

Charlotte B. Griffin, mayor of Bear Grass, told another story about Mozella's death that she heard from Simon Gardner, Mozella's last child. Simon and Charlotte's father, Mr. Buie Bailey, were good friends. She said that Simon told her that his mother died when she learned that he had been caught making moonshine.

Mozella married Joseph H. Davenport, age 25, (born in February 1870) from Washington County, North Carolina, on January 15, 1895, at the courthouse in Williamston. Mozella was 18. The 1900 census listed a J.F. Davenport and Mozella Davenport, and at that time they had one child, Samuel S. Davenport who was born in June 1899. My mother, Icelene Davenport, was born Sept. 9, 1902. These were the only two children from this union.

When I was a boy I remember going with mom to visit a Joe Sammy Davenport in Bethel, North Carolina, who was sick at the time. My mom called him Uncle Joe Sammy, indicating that he was her brother and my uncle. Not until 2006 was I able to confirm that indeed Joseph Samuel Davenport was by mother's brother.

In February 2006 I visited with James Davenport in Greenville, North Carolina, one of nine children born to Joe Sammy and his wife Alice Rawls. Eight of the children lived. James told me that Mozella and Joseph Davenport divorced (year unknown), and that Joseph took Joe Sammy and Mozella took Icelene. I have been unable to find a divorce decree that may shed some light on such an unusual arrangement. However, James noted that it was not Joseph Davenport that raised Joe Sammy but Joseph's mother. Joseph left the county and was not seen again until many years later when one of Joe Sammy's daughters found him living somewhere in the Edenton area and in very poor health. He said Joe Sammy let his dad live with them until he died in the mid-1940s. He said his grandfather died sitting on the front porch of someone's home in Oak City, North Carolina. They believe he died of a stroke or heart attack.

Born June 20, 1896, Joe Sammy died June 5, 1962, at Duke Hospital in Durham, North Carolina. He had suffered many years with arthritis, but the cause of his death is listed on the death certificate as upper GI bleeding. He was buried in the Bethel Cemetery.

Mozella's obituary does not mention the marriage to Davenport. Her obituary noted that she was first married to J.E. Moore, to whom her obituary attributes one child, Icelene. This is incorrect. There is no record of her marrying a J.E. Moore, but there are records of her marriage to Joseph Davenport and to William T. Gardner.

Mozella was married to William Thomas Gardner, who had one child, Major Thomas Gardner, by a previous marriage to Arvenia A. Gurganus Gardner. Arvenia died January 10, 1895. I believe this was Mozella's second and only other marriage.

Mozella and William Thomas Gardner were married on September 4, 1907, at the home of M.A. Webb by J.A. Lilley, justice of the peace. Witnesses were H.L. Rogerson, R.G. Rogerson and Ben Ward. Thomas was 53 and Mozella was 30. Thomas and Mozella had four children:

Noah Edmund, March 4, 1909 to September 5, 1959, age 50

Mary Emily Gardner Fleming, June 14, 1914 to December 14, 2000, age 86; the birth certificate on file in Williamston lists her first name as Marry, which is incorrect.

Daniel Mayo, September 17, 1917 to April 30, 1930, age 12

Simon Tilman, May 25, 1918 to October 27, 1991, age 73

Aunt Mary said there was another child, sex unknown, that died when it was only a couple of weeks old. A birth certificate or grave marker could not be found for this child. Thomas Gardner died February 8, 1933, at the age of 78.

Mary said that a couple of weeks before he died, Daniel watched his mother bury a pig. The boy told his mom he did not want to be put in the ground like that.

Mozella was buried with her husband Thomas in the Thomas Gardner Cemetery located on a farm on Tar Landing Road, west of Jamesville. From Highway 64, take Reason Road to Tar Landing Road and turn right. The graveyard is located about 100 yards on the right.

An obituary on page 1 of *The Enterprise* of Mr. Gardner's death indicated he had been married three times. I could not find any record of the third marriage. His obituary stated that he was survived by his wife, Mozella, and four children. Those four children were Noah, Mary, Simon and his son Major Gardner by his wife Arvenia. My mother, Icelene, was not mentioned as a stepdaughter. She retained the name Davenport. Major Gardner was born January 6, 1888, and he died on June 5, 1975. The 1910 census for Mozella and Thomas listed the following children: Noah, 1; Icelene, 7; and Major, 19; it was difficult to make out the spelling of this name, but it had to be Major even though his age should have been listed as 22 and not 19.

Mom's First Marriage and Children

Icelene Davenport was married to Raleigh (also called Riley) Columbus Bailey on January 1, 1922. He was born February 12, 1870, and died on March 28, 1926, at the age of 56. Raleigh was 42 days shy of his 52nd birthday and Icelene was 19 when they were married. This was his second marriage. His obituary indicates that he had six children by a previous marriage. The marriage license of Icelene and Raleigh lists Icelene as "Isolene Davenport." Children born to Raleigh and Icelene:

Kathleen Bailey, November 30, 1922 to November 21, 1995, age 72

Hilma Gray Bailey, born October 19, 1924

Raleigh had six children by his first wife: Lon, Hattie May, Thelma Lu, Buddy, Hugh M., and Lena Harrison.

When Raleigh died, Icelene gave Dennis Bailey permission to be the administrator of his estate. Bailey's real estate was valued at $2,000.00 and personal property at $400.00. For his services, Dennis charged $800.00, or one-third of the entire estate. The remaining $1,600.00 was to be divided between Raleigh's wife Icelene, his six children by his first marriage and two daughters by Icelene. They each received about $170.00.

Mom's Second Marriage and Children

On November 22, 1931, Icelene married William F. Barber. He was 35 days shy of his 55th birthday and she was 29. Children from this union:

Dallas H. Barber, born April 19, 1933

Mary M. Barber, born May 25, 1935

Jasper E. Barber, born November 9, 1938

Lester H. Barber, born May 16, 1940; committed suicide May 16, 2003, at the trailer in which he lived about 200 yards on the right from the end of Frank Barber Road.

Apparently a birth certificate was never filed on Lester and on July 6, 1957, Icelene signed a delayed birth certificate for him, which was needed before he could enter the U.S. Marine Corps. She signed her name Icelene on this certificate.

Miss Icelene, as she was affectionately called, died at home in her sleep March 24, 1967. No autopsy was performed, but it was believed the cause of death was a stroke or heart attack. She died with a smile on her face. She loved kids and raised a bunch of them and so it was appropriate that Lester's son Marty was sleeping with her the night she died.

It her obituary, her maiden name was listed as Gardner. Her name on Lester's delayed birth certificate is listed as "Icelean Davenport Barber," but she signed her first name Icelene. She never took on the name Gardner, which indicates she was not officially adopted into the Gardner family.

Total Number of Children

Two by her first husband Raleigh C. Bailey

Four by her second husband Frank Barber

Total: 6

The Barbers, Webbs and Slavery

A question that I pondered for many years is whether the Barber or Webb families owned slaves. I have not found any evidence to indicate that either family ever owned or was involved in owning slaves in whole or in part.

In Martin County in 1860 there were 4,309 slaves who were owned by 344 families. There were 551 free blacks living in the county. There were 5,435 whites living in Martin County in 1860. This means that just 15.8 percent of the whites in the county owned slaves. These figures are from the 1962 Tobacco Edition of *The Enterprise*.

The 1870 census was the first to list the names of black people. Before the slaves were freed, they did not have last names. Many took on the last names of their owners while others took on names of those responsible for liberating them. None of the blacks listed in the 1870 census took on the name of Barber or Webb.

The Barbers, Webbs and the Civil War

Henry Barber served in the Civil War, and I suspect he was drafted rather than being a volunteer. There is no record of anyone in the Webb family from Martin County serving in the Confederate Army.

Other Barbers in Martin County

Only one other family of Barbers appear on census reports from the 1800s and early 1900s. In the 1870 census, Benjamin F. Barber, 31, and Penny R., 30, are listed along with the following children: Katie, 10; Roena V., 8; Julia, 4; John T., 2; and Magdalene, 3 months. He was a preacher, and I suspect he was related to Henry

Barber in some way and it is quite possible that my grandfather Benjamin Barber was named after him. However, this is the only census report that lists this family, and I suspect that he moved on before the 1880 census was taken, but to where I do not know. My uncle Clyde Barber was a preacher and my nephew Paul Barber, Dennis and Essie's son, was a preacher. Also, Chubby Barber, Dennis and Essie Barber's grandson and my great nephew is a preacher. There could be others in the family in this profession that I am not aware of.

The Family Tree

Oh, my! What one can learn from a tree!
Standing naked in a winter storm
With just one leaf still hanging on

Suddenly, the lonely leaf is gone.
As the wind takes it to a new destination,
I am left with a terrifying realization!

I, too, am but a leaf on my family tree
And soon I'll be the departee!

ABOUT THE AUTHOR

Jasper (Jay) Earl Barber was the 21st child born to William Frank Barber and the fifth child born to Icelene Davenport Barber.

He was born November 9, 1938. It was a great day to be born in America. But it was not a great day in Germany. It was Kristallnacht in Deutschland, the night in which Adolf Hitler and his Nazi party began their attack on Jews just because they were Jews. Before that night of horror ended—it lasted until May 8, 1945, when World War II officially ended--more than six million innocent Jews would be exterminated, mostly in gas chambers. His only memory of this war was the funeral he attended at Reddicks Grove Baptist Church of a soldier who fought in that war.

He attended school in Jamesville, North Carolina, from 1945 to 1956. In 1956 he farmed 100 acres of land and tried to go to school, too. He could not serve two masters. He quit the 11th grade in November and on December 28 enlisted in the United States Air Force.

He remained in the Air Force until October 1, 1980, retiring with 24 years of service as a senior master sergeant. During that time he served in public relations, recruiting and as an historian. He attended Martin Community College in Williamston, North Carolina, from 1981 to 1982 and East Carolina University in nearby Greenville from 1982 to 1984. He graduated Magna Cum Laude in May, 1984, with a Bachelor of Science Degree in English, the only child of Frank or Icelene Barber to graduate from college.

In August 1984 he accepted a job with the public affairs office at Seymour Johnson Air Force Base in Goldsboro, North Carolina. He became the deputy chief of the 4th Fighter Wing Public Affairs Office and served in that position until retiring a second time on March 1, 2001.

He married Mary Jane Rogers in Brewer, Maine, on October 2, 1959. They have two sons: Dean and Larry; a granddaughter, Kelly, and a grandson, Chad. They reside in Goldsboro, North Carolina.